In a past era of turbulence akin to our own,
Abraham Lincoln said: "I believe the Bible is
the best gift God has ever given to man."
Today men seek a clear, authoritative word to
bring meaning and harmony out of the tumult
which engulfs them. Thus there is a
resurgent interest in the Bible, but coupled
with this is a confusion as to what
the Book actually teaches. **A Look at the Book** is
not only a study of the Bible—but it guides
the reader to study the Bible for himself.
And it focuses on the one unifying point of all
the Scriptures: the person of Jesus Christ.

A LOOK AT THE BOOK

A LOOK AT THE BOOK

daily devotions and studies in the Bible and what it says about itself

By Manford George Gutzke

A Division of G/L Publications
Glendale, California, U.S.A.

©Copyright 1969 by Manford George Gutzke

Printed in U.S.A.

Published by
Regal Books Division, G/L Publications
Glendale, California 91205, U.S.A.

Library of Congress Catalog Card No. 69-16632

Contents

A study guide is available for use with this book. Consult your supplier or the publisher.

This book may be used as an elective Sunday School course, or for Sunday evening fellowships or midweek Bible study classes.

Foreword

In a world overflowing with books, the Bible stands in a class by itself. Exalted by the veneration of the centuries, it has also been banned and burned. Best loved of books, it is also the most hated and feared. It makes the greatest claims of any book, and it backs them up in demonstrations of power and influence. For the Bible is unique in that it speaks with a living voice to one generation as well as to another. And it speaks to everyman with astonishing insight and penetration. It exposes needs while at the same time supplying answers.

In an age when so much of the literary output suffers moral pollution, it is heartening to note a reawakening of interest in what the Bible says. For the Bible is not an end in itself. The words of the apostle John in describing the purpose of his Gospel may properly be applied to the whole Bible: "These are written, that ye might believe that Jesus is the Christ, the Son of God; and that believing ye might have life through his name."

This goal is kept in the forefront in *A Look at the Book*, which provides a study-book introduction to the Scriptures. Their authority, their various literary forms, their unity through the person of Jesus Christ—these are some of the aspects of the Bible treated in these pages in such a way that the study of the Bible is not only encouraged and taught, but is also exemplified. Particularly stressed are the spiritual nourishment and practical guidance afforded by the Word of the eternal God, who has seen the end from the beginning and beyond whose sovereign control the events of this world cannot go.

How to Use This Book

This is a daily devotional and study workbook. Here are some suggestions for its most profitable use.

Study the Scriptures daily, using the Bible readings in this book as your guide. There are Bible readings for every day of the week. Always begin by asking the Holy Spirit to guide you and give you a personal message for the day. Read with a pencil in your hand and record your responses to the questions asked.

On the last page of each chapter you will find "Make a Decision." Read this after you have completed the daily studies for the chapter. Determine to apply what you have learned during the week in your Bible study. *Develop the habit of searching the Scriptures for the solutions to life's problems.* The last pages of this volume contain a list of books for further reading which will enrich your study as you refer to them.

It is suggested that you use a notebook as you study, to record your thoughts, questions and answers concerning the passages of Scripture you have read.

CHAPTER 1

Written for Us

Bible reading for this week: I Corinthians 10:1-12

There are two common ways to learn something— find out for yourself or be told by someone who knows.

Since God is invisible, no man can "by searching find out God." Then the only way for a man to learn about the will of God is to be told.

The works of God are manifest, being seen in the stars above. But the promises of God would never be known if He had not revealed them in His Word.

God dealt with Abraham and with His seed in a special way to show all men His will. Then God inspired "holy men of God" to write "as they were moved by the Holy Ghost." Thus the Scriptures were written for us.

1. For Our Guidance
Deuteronomy 5:1,22

Living is like going somewhere. Each day I step out into new territory where I have never been before. As I go from one thing to another I have all kinds of things happen to me, both good and bad. I cannot help but want only good to happen.

I soon find out that things happen differently when I do differently. If there are two ways to go there will be a difference in what happens to me if I go one way or the other.

I am the same person and I always want only things good for me. But what happens to me on one road is not the same as what happens when I take the other road. The road I take makes a difference in what happens to me. Also there is a difference in what each road leads to. I cannot take any road and get where I want to go. I must take the right road if I want to reach the right place.

How will I know which road to take? Somebody must show me. The person who can show me is the one who knows where the roads go, and what will happen to me when I go on this road or that road.

If I want the blessing of God in my life I need to be guided by someone who knows what it is to be blessed of God. Such men were the prophets. They were men who knew God, and were blessed of

God; so they could lead others to God.

Also they needed to be led by the Holy Spirit of God so they could say the things that would be helpful to us. They did not know us, but God knew what we would need, and He could lead them to write what we needed to know.

What are some of the good things I might want in my life? In what ways could God affect my experience to help me get these things? Why would I need guidance to help me get the help of God? What book would I normally read and study to find out the will of God? What would I have to do if I wanted the guidance of God in my life? Would knowing how God led Abraham, Moses, Isaac, Paul and others in the Bible be helpful for me to know how I could expect God to lead me? Why?

2. For Our Instruction
Nehemiah 8:5-8

To follow an established procedure requires instruction. Any procedure has its own design or pattern which is different, and must be learned by anyone who might want to follow it successfully.

God is a person and by His very nature requires a certain procedure on the part of any human being who would come to Him. No man in himself can ever conceive what that would be. "Eye hath not seen, nor ear heard, neither have entered into the heart of man, the things which God hath prepared for them that love him" (I Corinthians 2:9). But

God can and has revealed these through His Spirit.

The Holy Spirit knows the deep things of God and He has revealed these things in the Scriptures. Thus the believer who studies the Bible will actually be instructed in the ways of God. That God would allow another to substitute Himself to bear the penalty for sin would never be known if God did not reveal this to be true. Sinners need to be told.

That the Son of God would offer Himself as a substitutionary sacrifice for me would never be thought of or believed if He did not say so Himself.

That God would accept the death of Jesus Christ instead of demanding my own death for my sins would never be believed if He did not reveal this in His Word.

In all such matters we need instruction and this is given to us in the Scriptures.

Where is the first place in the Bible where man was instructed to bring sacrifice? Who was the first priest appointed to perform worship for believers? How did Moses know what the Ten Commandments should include? How did Moses know what Aaron should do as high priest? How did Aaron know how to offer the various offerings? How did Israel know how to arrange the camp when they stopped anywhere (Numbers 2:34)? How did Moses know how the tabernacle should be set up (Exodus 40:16)? If you wanted to know God's will for you where would you look? Could you expect to get help? Why? To know how to die where would one look?

3. For Our Warning
Jeremiah 36:2,3,21-23

Living is always a risky business and sometimes
there is real peril. Whenever a road has real danger
in it, the usual thing is to put up a sign of warning.
Every cross country traveler has reason to be grate-
ful for the thoughtfulness of others who warn him
about danger he will meet.

Much happens to a man who travels that could
be spoken of as "providence." The Christian believes in the providence of God and expects to
receive warning when he approaches danger.

Some of the danger will arise from circumstances
and therefore the Christian will try to be alert and
to watch at all times. But some of the danger will
be the result of his own conduct. He may not
realize that what he does will bring results, and so
God warns him about what will happen if he does
or if he does not act in certain ways.

It is so very important to keep in mind that "God
is not mocked: whatsoever a man soweth that shall
he also reap." It was for this very reason that the
Ten Commandments were given. By the law is the
knowledge of sin.

Warnings do not make it certain a man will do
right, but they can keep him from doing wrong.
The warning signs on the highway have not the
power to keep cars on the road, but they are
helpful to drivers who want to avoid disaster.

"Poison" signs on bottles of drugs have no
efficacy to prevent foolish carelessness, but they can

be useful in saving lives for those who want to be careful, but who might be ignorant of the danger involved.

Why could a person look to God for help in any situation that might arise any day in his life? Why could we count on the Lord to guide us in any particular problem that we face? We think of God as a living God. How does this relate to his having a plan for my life or your life? How could a real Christian miss the guidance of the Lord? How could a Christian miss the warning of the Lord? How could a Christian miss the real joy and blessing of the Lord? Look up the life story of your favorite Old Testament character and see how he received guidance from God. How does this help you to understand better how to expect guidance from God?

4. For Our Comfort
Romans 15:4

Suffering and loss come easily in this world. Especially is this true when a soul seeks to obey the will of God. Jesus of Nazareth was without sin, living a perfect life, but He suffered unto death. "The servant is not greater than his lord." The Lord Jesus warned His disciples that if these things could happen to a green tree, it would be even worse for those that were dry.

It would appear that God would have men learn that this world is not desirable as a permanent home. In spite of all diligence and competence "in the world ye shall have tribulation." The Bible teaches that "man is born unto trouble, as the sparks fly upward." But Jesus assured his followers, "Be of good cheer; I have overcome the world."

Death is an enemy that cannot be evaded, but Jesus Christ has secured for His own followers victory over death. God can and will raise the dead. Death hath lost its sting. The grave has been robbed of its victory. The believer can face death with composure because Jesus Christ was raised from the dead.

Suffering the loss of this world's goods is more than matched by the joys of the world to come (Hebrews 10:34).

Even the distress of being rejected by man fades away in the joy of belonging to the Father.

When the missionary, Dr. Vinson, was about to be shot by bandits, his quiet composure puzzled his executioners. "Aren't you afraid," they asked. "Afraid of what," said Dr. Vinson. "The moment you kill me here I will be standing in the presence of the King."

How could a young wife dying with a terminal disease, be comforted as she thought of leaving her husband and baby? How could a teen-age girl who has been seriously injured in a car wreck find comfort? How could you comfort a young man who has been refused the hand of the girl he loved? What Scripture would you use to comfort a young football star who suddenly found himself confined to a sick bed with no hope of ever walking again? Why would you use this specific passage? How could a person be comforted who has been falsely accused by his friend? How would Matthew 26:47, 48,59, and 60 help?

5. For Our Learning
I Corinthians 10:11

Benefits in living depend on what I know. It is not enough that I work or even that I work hard. I must work wisely in order to get good results. Putting beans into the ground is not enough to get a crop of beans. I must know when to plant and how to plant and how to care for growing beans if I want to harvest beans in my garden.

Spiritual benefits also depend upon my acting intelligently. I need to come to God that I may be blessed, but this is something I must learn to do in the right way.

Because the things of the soul are invisible and are not of this world, I cannot find them by looking around in the natural world I can see. My spiritual life is directly involved with God. Just what I must do and how I may do it, must be revealed to me by the Holy Spirit who was given to lead me into fellowship with God.

"All Scripture is given by inspiration of God, and is profitable for doctrine, for reproof, for correction, for instruction in righteousness" (II Timothy 3:16). It would seem that the written Word of God is the Sword of the Spirit, so that I could learn the ways of God by reading and by studying the Bible.

When the risen Jesus of Nazareth wanted His disciples to understand what His resurrection really meant, he "opened their understanding that they might understand the Scriptures."

Paul told the Corinthian Christians that things happened to Israel and were then recorded in Scripture so that later generations might have these things as examples from which to learn the truth.

If a farmer wanted to learn how to raise wheat where would he look? If a doctor wanted to know the cure of a particular disease where would he look? If a man wanted to know about God where might he look? How did Abraham learn about God (Genesis 12:1)? How did Cornelius learn about God (Acts 10)? How did the Ethiopian eunuch learn about God (Acts 8:26-36)? How does the little Chinese boy learn about God? How did you learn about God? Inasmuch as the Bible is food for the soul of the child of God, why do you think it is read so little? How often do you read the Bible?

6. For Our Salvation
II Timothy 3:15-17

The Bible is directly involved in our salvation. "By grace are ye saved through faith" is the wonderful truth. And it is further true that "Faith cometh by hearing, and hearing by the Word of God." It has always been to the glory of God that it pleased God by the foolishness of preaching to save them that believe. Where the Bible has been taught

9

and known, souls have believed and have been saved.

Salvation is the work of God just as creation is the work of God. And both are by His Word. "Through faith we understand that the worlds were framed by the Word of God" (Hebrews 11:3). And as Peter says "by the word of God the heavens were of old, and the earth standing out of the water and in the water" (II Peter 3:5). Paul says of the Holy Scriptures that they "are able to make thee wise unto salvation through faith which is in Christ Jesus" (II Timothy 3:15).

Peter goes so far as to say that the believer is born again not of corruptible seed, but of incorruptible, by the Word of God (I Peter 1:23). He then goes on to say in his second epistle that in the Scriptures "are given unto us exceeding great and precious promises: that by these ye might be partakers of the divine nature, having escaped the corruption that is in the world through the lust" (II Peter 1:4).

The Bible has the same relation to salvation as the acorn has to the oak tree. All the "oakness" of the oak is in the acorn. No matter how many thousand leaves the oak tree may have and each one different from all others, all these leaves will be oak leaves because of the acorn from which the tree grew. Even so with salvation and the Bible. All saved souls will be like Christ because of the Bible from whence they derived their faith.

Since the Bible is the most important book a man can read what should be the position of the Bible in the Sunday School departments? What should be its place in the pulpit? What should be the position of the Bible in youth work? What should be the position of the Bible in the missionary endeavors? Write out Matthew 28:19,20. What does this verse mean to your personally? Would a person visiting your Sunday School class hear enough about Jesus Christ to be saved? Why, or why not?

7. For Our Eternal Life
Revelation 22:16-21

Eternal life is the life of God. This life is different from man not only in that it lives forever, and will never die; but also in its very nature. It is without sin. When Jesus of Nazareth said, "He that believeth in me hath eternal life," He meant much more than that such a person would live forever; He meant that such a person had in Him the life of God.

Just as the life of Adam is begotten in any human being in a biological way because of the seed of man, so the life of God is begotten in any believer in a spiritual way because of the Word of God. Because God is eternally living and His Word is eternally His own, when the promise is received and obeyed God makes it actual and real. The new creature is begotten and that person is in reality a child of God.

Much of the truth of eternal life lies beyond our grasp, but one thing we can know for sure, the new born child of God is begotten by the Word of God and the Spirit of God.

Also we know that as a new born babe he should "desire the sincere milk of the word" that he "might grow thereby" (I Peter 2:2).

That which is in the Christian which is spiritual and comes from God comes in by and through the Scriptures, the Word of God.

In the Bible we have the food that keeps the Christian alive, and helps him to be strong.

How would you explain the peace and serenity of spirit Christians have exhibited in the face of murder by their enemies? If a preacher spends nearly all his time expounding on some social issue or current event what would likely happen to the young man who comes to church seeking God? What would happen to the souls in despair who come as their last resort? What would likely happen to the children who are raised in that church? If you as a teacher of the men's Bible class wanted to be sure you have your students understand what it means to have the life of God within their own souls, what Scripture would you use to get this point across? Why would you choose these Bible verses? How important is the Bible to you personally? Do you believe it? Do you read it? Why, or why not?

Make a Decision

It always gives us great pleasure to receive a personal letter containing good news. It changes our whole day, even our outlook on life gets brighter, at least for the time being. In a very real sense God's Word, the Bible, is God's personal letter to you. This letter contains the most wonderful news the human ear will ever hear. God has so arranged it that you, a sinner, far from God, may come to Him, receive salvation and be blessed as the days go by. This is for you. This is the message of the Bible. It can be yours now.

CHAPTER 2

God Said It—Man Wrote It

Bible reading for this week: II Peter 1:20,21

Speaking any word is actually a creative act. This is not always clearly seen, as when a person is simply repeating what someone else has said. Such is more like talking rather than saying anything. When we refer to the Word of God we mean: what God is saying.

The problem of ever knowing what God has said is caused by the fact that He does not enter into popular, or public conversation. Only certain qualified persons hear what He says and then transmit it to men. "God, who at sundry times and in divers manners spake in time past unto the fathers by the prophets" (Hebrews 1:1). As God says it, it is creative; as man writes it, it is authoritative.

1. In Creation
Hebrews 11:3

"In the beginning God created the heaven and the earth" (Genesis 1:1). To create, in this context, is to bring into being something that never existed before. It means to produce something out of nothing. The Bible tells how it happened. God spoke and the earth stood fast.

The created world shows a rational design. All aspects of things were present at the creation. When the world was projected into being by God it had the natural processes it has now. Their adequacy which makes them all fit together is a tribute to the wisdom of God as Creator.

The speaking of a word is a creative act. Before it was spoken the word did not exist. In saying, there is choice and design. The formulation of thought can go on in infinite variety as long as it is not uttered. Even as we speak we realize we are expressing only one of the endless possibilities. To say anything is to set out in recognizable fashion the one thing we decided to establish in articulation.

After it has been said, it can be repeated. Now it can be noted and studied. Something of the intention and of the mind of the speaker can be learned by others who hear the word and consider it.

Apparently, speaking does not require vocal utterance. A man can give his word by nodding his head. But if the word is to be known by others it must be translated into the language others understand.

The Bible tells us that God spoke in times past to the fathers by the prophets. To hear what God would say and to tell that to the people in their language was the very function assigned to Moses (Deuteronomy 5:27).

What is the difference between "to create" (as used in Genesis 1:1) and "to make"? Why is it so very important to believe that God created the universe and all therein? How does the doctrine of creation out of nothing contradict pantheism? What would be the effect of a minister's preaching if he doubted the creation story of the Bible was true? How could a girl from a truly Christian home be able to face a young biology professor, who denies that God created the world, without losing her faith? If you doubted any part of the Bible how could you believe any other part of it? Explain Hebrews 11:3. What does this verse mean to your personal faith?

2. In Sending Light
Genesis 1:3

Light is one of the elements in the natural world that is not fully understood. No one knows what light is. Men know something of how it acts and what it does. But the actual grasp of what it is has never been realized.

Apparently light moves through space. Men have been able to measure the speed of light. And men have noted that light travels in waves, which may be thought of as undulations in the stream of energy which at this specific speed becomes light.

The Bible records a simple statement: "And God said, Let there be light: and there was light" (Genesis 1:3). Here it is plainly recorded that God spoke the word and light shone. Paul refers to this when he writes: "For God, who commanded the light to shine out of darkness . . ." (II Corinthians 4:6).

This origin of light in the expressed will of God would not be known to man if it had not been recorded when holy men of God spoke as they were moved by the Holy Ghost. That light is a form of energy can be seen in the effect of light in the natural world. All power belongs to God, and light is something God is doing.

There is a profound meaning in the Scripture, I am the Light of the world. This same truth was expressed when John wrote, "That was the true Light, which lighteth every man that cometh into the world" (John 1:9). In the same passage Christ is spoken of as the Word of God. In a sense, the Word and the Light are one.

What does it mean to you that God spake and there was light? What does this tell you about God? *Natural light* is so very important to plants. They need it in order to grow. How is the Bible like light in its effect on our souls? As a child do you recall being afraid in the dark and how glad you were when someone turned the light on? How does this compare to the soul until he hears the gospel? What does "out of darkness into his marvelous light" mean (I Peter 2:9)? List all the passages you can find in the Bible which refer to the Bible or Jesus

17

Christ as light. What new truth have you learned from this study? What decision has today's lesson caused you to make?

3. In Giving the Law
Exodus 20:1

The law of God is eternal. But it was not always known to man. On Mount Sinai Moses received the Ten Words on the tables of stone that we speak of as the Ten Commandments. Writing the Law on these tablets of stone did not mean any new thing. The only aspect that was new was that they were written.

It was always a sin to kill another man. When Cain killed Abel he transgressed the law of God, and was judged because of his sin. It was always wrong to steal. It was always a sin to take God's name in vain. But when these words were written it was easier for man to know when he was doing wrong.

Going 80 miles an hour around a mountain curve is always dangerous. Putting up signs stating the speed limit to be 35 miles an hour is a help to the traveler who may not be aware of the danger. The warning signs do not create the danger. The danger is in the grade and the road. But the signs alert the driver to the peril which is there and always was there.

So it is with the law of God. God is in Himself holy and will not condone sin. The law of God is grounded in the unchangeable nature of God. But the writing of it in the language of men is for the sake of men.

Moses did not invent or originate any part of the law. His writings are for the help of men so that they may know what is sin before God.

Does the label on a bottle of poison make the contents poison? Why put the label on the bottle of poison? Why put up the sign "detour" when the bridge is out? Why put up the quarantine sign when a child in the house has measles? Why did God express the law in human language? Why is reading the Bible so very important to the unbeliever? to the believer? What does it mean to say "the law of God is eternal"? Since having the law written in human language was a blessing from God to man, how does it help to have it right before our eyes? How can the law bring us to Jesus Christ (Galatians 3:24)?

4. In Instructing the Prophets
Ezekiel 3:11

God spoke unto the fathers by the prophets. People in the public have never been able to hear the Word of God directly. God has always communicated His will to His people by chosen men who came to know His will by close fellowship and communion with Him, and who then served by translating this message into such language as the people could understand.

19

The prophets were not wise men who understood the problems of the people and were clever in discovering solutions. Actually the situations in which problems arose were of such a nature that only the hand of God Himself could effect a solution. The prophets were men to whom God revealed what He would do to help His people, and the conditions under which this help would be given.

Thus the prophet would come to the people and say, "Thus saith the Lord." Whenever there was unconfessed sin commonly practiced by the people, the prophet would point this out and call the people to repent. Many times the prophets were rejected and even killed because of popular resentment to their stern messages. But of course this would not change the truth.

The prophet's mission was to tell the people what God had in mind. He would tell them about their sin and call upon them to repent. He would tell them of coming judgment and call upon them to turn to God. He would tell them of God's eternal purpose and urge them to believe (II Peter 1:20,21).

What does the word "prophet" mean? What does the Bible mean when it calls Jesus of Nazareth "a prophet"? How could you consider your pastor a prophet in a Biblical sense? In the Bible God called His prophets unto Him personally for instruction and guidance. By what means does He call His servants today and how does He instruct them and guide them into His will? If you are a Christian and need specific guidance and help from the Lord, what can you do? Tell in your own words of a time in your life when you needed special help from the Lord and how He gave you the help you needed. What changes in your own spiritual life do you feel you want to make after this study?

5. In Revealing the Truth
Daniel 12:4

God is a living Being, almighty in power and infinite in wisdom, who has plans of His own for His creation and His creatures. The Bible does not say that God made the world and put man in it to make out the best he could manage. Actually He knows all things and sees even the sparrow fall to the ground. He has His own will for all that happens.

Man does not know everything. He does not understand everything around him, and he certainly does not fully know the past nor can he foresee the future. Since the will of God is in control it would be very important for man to know that will and to cooperate in it as far as possible. Man cannot by searching find out God, so for guidance man is dependent upon God's revelation of His will.

The will of God is eternal. Long before anything happens the course of the action is already known to God. Some of God's will is revealed to His servants through His Word, and then is written in the Scriptures. The man who reads and studies the Bible can know what the will of God is, and can respond to it in faith. Such persons will be blessed in their obedience.

The will of God was revealed by His Spirit to His servants, who then wrote to the people of God such messages as would convey the knowledge of His will to all who would be obedient.

How could I come to know the will of God? What evidence can we see that God did not make the world and then leave man to do the best he could? If a man decides he will give his life over to God to let him order his affairs, what can he expect will happen? Since it is impossible to come to know God apart from the Bible, what place should the Bible have in the ministry of the church? Are there any Christians where the Bible has not been? Why? What does this show about the Bible? What does the saying "the Bible tells a man how to live and how to die" mean? Write out Psalm 119:11. What does this verse mean to you personally?

6. In Revealing the Meaning of Visions
Revelation 1:19

The will of God is not revealed to all men in the same way. Some men are not worthy to be shown what God will do (Matthew 7:6; II Peter 2:22; Jude 18,19). Thus in the Bible there are portions which cannot be understood by such men. But these portions can be seen in their truth when interpreted by the Holy Spirit to believers—those regenerated by the Spirit.

Several times in the history of Israel the people

of God were prisoners in the hands of their enemies. At such times the revelation of the Word of God came in visions, as it did to Ezekiel, Daniel, and John while he was on the Isle of Patmos. The meaning of these visions was later given and recorded in Scripture. A study of such Scripture will reveal the meaning of the vision, which at first was hidden in the figurative symbolism of the vision.

It would seem that the full meaning of the vision can only be recognized when the particular situation for which it was given is brought into focus.

The several illustrations of such interpretations in Scripture will help to show an important principle for the understanding of any part of the Bible. When the Scripture is brought into the context of the spiritual situation for which it was written, the true meaning of the revelation can be seen.

All of this means above everything else that each part of the Bible is meaningful, and that truth can be seen when Scripture is compared with Scripture, and is related to the actual spiritual experience of the believer who reads the Bible.

During wartime, what means are used to see that the enemy cannot figure out what is going on? Sometimes in Bible history, God's people were in enemy hands; what special means did God use at such times to get His message to His people? Why was it important that the enemy not find out what God was telling His people? How can we today benefit from these messages written in symbolism? Is the message different from other parts of the Bible literature? What does this tell you about the Bible? Has this study increased your confidence in

7. In Producing Results
Isaiah 55:11

"For the word of God is quick, and powerful, and sharper than any twoedged sword" (Hebrews 4:12). The Bible is different from any other book, in that it has dynamic power. Because it is the Word of the living God it can actually produce results in those who read and heed.

Nicodemus indicated he had confidence in Jesus of Nazareth as a teacher come from God because of the works which He did. By the same sign the Bible has a right to claim the confidence of anyone.

Consideration of the connection between the phenomena of Christianity and the teaching of the Bible will show that the Bible is the one source on earth that is constant in the history of anything that is Christian. To this day the undeniable results which follow the teaching of the Bible continue to commend the authenticity of the message (Acts 4:14).

The hearing of the message of the Bible generates faith among those who listen (Romans 10:17).

Confidence in the Scriptures is the ground for peace of soul among those who believe (Psalm 119:165).

Hope in the future and in the promises of God is to be found in those who read and believe the Bible (Romans 15:4).

When hid in the heart the Scriptures actually keep a believer from sinning against God (Psalm 119:11).

If you were choosing a doctor, what recommendation would you pay attention to? If you had been given a prescription for medicine, what is the first thing you would want to know? What is the greatest recommendation given about the Bible? What is the one result that is surely to happen if one reads the Bible with desire to know the truth? Write as many statements as you can which indicate the Bible to be the Word of God. How is each one like what Jesus of Nazareth did while He was here? What new truth have you learned from this study? Write out Hebrews 4:12. What does this verse say to you personally?

Make a Decision

The Bible, God's revelation to man, tells man about God, what He wills for man, what He will accept and what He will reject. It is absolute. He is unchanging. Whatsoever He says is final.

Man would have never known about God had God not chosen to reveal Himself. Thus the Bible is of utmost importance. Wherever the Bible is accepted and honored there you will find Christians. The Christian is in the world but not of the world and he is kept by the power of God. Is this power yours? If not, are you ready to make it yours *now?*

CHAPTER 3

It's the Truth

Bible reading for this week: II Timothy 3:14-17

A person who doesn't know about things is always in danger of being deceived. He does not understand what he sees and he cannot be sure of the meaning of what he hears. Some are tempted to fall into the error of accepting what sounds good, and this of course can be disastrous.

Without words we cannot think, and words are given to us by others. But early in our lives we learn that what some people say cannot be accepted as true or valid. Usually we learn to identify people in our home, family or neighborhood that can be trusted to tell the truth. Paul reminded Timothy that he had learned the Scriptures from just such reliable persons, so they could be accepted as the truth.

1. It Is Certified
Isaiah 8:20

In all the affairs of men, deceit and error are never as rampant as in matters which are involved in a man's faith in his God. This is not because matters of religious faith are necessarily evil, but rather because these very important matters deal with invisible realities. The matters of the spiritual world are so very important, but at the same time they are unseen. This means that a man will seek to know but that also he can easily be deceived just because the realities are obscure and unseen. It is of utmost importance that a man have some guidance to help him judge what he is to accept as true.

Throughout history, many have come to know God in a real personal way. These have been able to help others know God's will. Such were Abraham, Isaac, Jacob, Joseph, Moses, Joshua, Gideon, Elijah, Isaiah among others in the Old Testament times, and Peter, James, John, Paul and others in the New Testament era. These men knew God and for the benefit of other men and later generations they wrote down some of their experiences and insights (II Peter 1:12-21) in the Scriptures.

The writings of Moses and other prophets of God were known as the Law and the testimony.

By the time of Isaiah false doctrine was already being preached, and error was being taught. To help sincere people recognize what could be accepted as true Isaiah urged them to compare what they were hearing with the Law and the testimony, and then told them plainly that any doctrine which differed from the writings of the holy men of God was simply not true.

The Law and the testimony could properly be taken as adequate to certify the truth of the gospel.

What would happen to any man who drank arsenic because it was labeled milk of magnesia? What difference would the label make? Why? What does the Bible say for the man who advocates "it does not matter what you believe if you are sincere"? What does Acts 4:12 mean in light of the above statement? What is the main reason that spiritual things are so hard to understand? Write out I Corinthians 2:8. In your own words tell what this verse means?

2. It is Effectual
Isaiah 55:11

Again and again some man would come to the people of God with a message which he claimed was sent from God. But not every man was true. There were false prophets who claimed to bring the true Word of God, but who were liars. This raised a problem with every messenger—was his message truly from God?

Moses knew that the people would have to face this problem, so he gave them a simple principle for their guidance (Deuteronomy 18:21,22). They were to note what happened after the message was delivered. If the word of the prophet came to pass he was truly sent of God; if the word of the prophet was not fulfilled then he spoke out of his own mind, and was a false prophet.

When Elijah prayed on Mount Carmel for fire to come down upon the altar he had prepared, he asked that God do this "that this people may know that thou art the Lord God," and "that I am thy servant, and that I have done all these things at thy word" (I Kings 18:36,37).

When Nicodemus came to Jesus of Nazareth by night he said, "Rabbi, we know that thou art a teacher come from God: for no man can do these miracles that thou doest, except God be with him" (John 3:2). His confidence in Jesus of Nazareth as a true servant of God was based, not upon what Jesus said, but upon the effectiveness of his ministry.

All this is true of the Scripture as the Word of God. Isaiah pointed out that it would accomplish what it was sent to do, because it was the Word of God (Isaiah 55:11).

Gamalial later pointed out that if anything were from God "ye cannot overthrow it" (Acts 5:39).

The effectiveness of the Bible is powerful evidence that it is from God.

A man's integrity is judged by the way he keeps his word. If he fails to keep it, we consider him to be dishonest and unreliable. Then what about God's Word—how should it be treated? Has the Bible ever once in its history, to the best of your knowledge, failed to do what it promised when it was obeyed? How do you determine whether a thing is true or not? What is the Word of God sent to do (John 16:8-11)? If you wanted to know if the water is hot what would you do? If you wanted to know if the Bible is true what would you do?

3. It Is Verified
Jeremiah 28:9

In the midst of confusion and doubt because so many contrary messages are set forth as the Word of God, the Bible tells of one condition which settles all argument. Jeremiah was opposed by another prophet called Hananiah. When Jeremiah warned the king that his disobedience to God would result in the destruction of his kingdom, Hananiah contradicted him and predicted peace. There was no way to establish the word of Jeremiah by any sort of argument, but Jeremiah told the king how he would know. If peace came as Hananiah predicted then he was telling the truth, but if destruction came then Hananiah was a liar. "The proof of the puddin' is in the eating thereof."

This is the one line of proof about the Bible that leaves a broad, clear conclusion about its being the Word of God. The Bible is not some recent idea lately formed and presented to the world. There has been plenty of time and wide range of opportunity to check the results of Bible teaching. Wherever the Word has been preached and received, it has resulted in like benefits and like results. The results have been good and the benefits have been enriching to all that were involved.

"Ask the man who owns one" was a famous

advertising slogan for a certain car some years ago. It is certainly the challenge which the Bible can put before the whole world. If anyone should really want to know about the significance of the Bible, the sensible, logical thing to do is "ask someone who believes it!"

What does "verified" mean? How would you know if a thing was verified or not? How could you show that the Bible is verified? If a thing was true could there be disapproving voices against it? Why? List as many reasons as you can which man gives for doubting the Bible? List as many reasons as you can for confidence in the Bible? What are your personal reasons for confidence in the Bible? Can you say "tried and proven" about the Bible? If not, what is hindering you?

4. It Is Permanent
Matthew 5:18

"For ever, O Lord, thy word is settled in heaven" (Psalm 119:89). The Bible is different from the writings of men in that it is always true and will be true forever. Today some say that the Bible is not relevant to this time, that it is outdated. It seems they have never read the Scriptures!

The truths set forth in the Bible are the truths about God who never changes. The message of the Bible is not limited to a specific nation or age. The very fact that the Bible deals with the things of God and of man's relation to God makes it of surpassing value for all people and all ages.

The things of the world change like the clouds in the sky, and the waves of the sea.

"Change and decay in all around I see.

O Thou who changest not, abide with me."

It is true that the Word of God when spoken and written has entered into this world of change, but despite the changeableness of man the Word of God as written by holy men of God as they were moved by the Holy Ghost is permanent.

Jesus of Nazareth made the declaration, "Till heaven and earth pass, one jot or one tittle shall in no wise pass from the law, till all be fulfilled" (Matthew 5:18). The jot and the tittle in the Hebrew alphabet are like the dotting of an "i" and the crossing of a "t." This is a way of emphasizing that the written Word will stand as it is throughout the duration of this world.

When the Word became flesh in Jesus of Nazareth, the eternal Word took on a temporal form which will never be any different. The life, death, burial and resurrection of Jesus Christ have become permanent truth forever.

Why is an earthquake such a terrorizing event? List five events which can bring about drastic changes in the natural world. List three things in the natural world which will never change as long as this world endures. Tell about an experience you had when someone changed his mind about something. What comfort is it that God never changes? What comfort is it that the Word of God never changes? What comfort is it that the way of salvation never changes?

5. It Is a Mirror
James 1:23

A mirror is often very unpopular. No boy with a dirty face wants to look into a mirror. If a man needs a shave or a hair cut he may not want to look into a mirror. Anyone who is untidy or unclean or unkempt will not want a mirror.

But the boy who wants to clean up will want a mirror! The man who wants to shave, to get his hair cut, will want a mirror. The young bride who wants to look her very best will want a mirror.

The Bible can serve as a mirror to the soul. Any man as he reads in the Bible will come across persons who seem to be just as he is/was/will be.

The Bible will reveal a man's innermost ideas and thoughts, and will show how these things will stand in the judgment of God.

This aspect of the Bible is unchangeable, and is often very unpopular. People seem to forget the Bible does not *move in* to change persons. It does *show* up anybody, any time.

Some people will not allow a thermometer in their room because they are sure it will cause the temperature to go up or down as the case may be.

In this way some will not read the Bible because it makes them feel bad. The truth probably is that they *are* bad and they just do not want to be reminded of the fact.

For anybody who does not want to change, the Bible could be embarrassing because his lack of desire to be different will show up as he reads the

Bible. However, the Bible in itself cannot change any man; it can show him the need and the remedy.

What benefit would a mirror be to the concert pianist? What value is the Xray to a healthy man? to the man with cancer? How is the Bible a mirror to the young high school student getting mixed up with a group whose members practice immoral relationships with each other? How is the Bible a mirror to the science student who is being confronted with atheistic ideas? How is the Bible a mirror to the young Christian? In what way is the Bible a mirror to the growing Christian? What changes could this lesson bring about in your life?

6. It Is Consistent
Acts 15:15

Difference and variety are common anywhere. One of the common disappointments in life is to see changes and contradictions everywhere. People change, so that many unhappy events occur because what was promised last month was not done this month and will be prevented from happening next month.

This condition has become so common that today only written and signed contracts generally have any significance. It is considered foolish to accept a man's word.

The Bible is entirely different. Not only is every word permanent but they do not contradict one another. All parts of the Bible belong together like

34

all parts of the human body. Though different in size and shape they are actually so fearfully and wonderfully made that they are all fitly joined together as a habitation of the Spirit.

This gives a very real sense of assurance and strength. For there is no fear of unexpected "interior collision" among the parts, but rather a common unity which gives health and harmony.

The fact that all parts agree with one another is further evidence that there is but one Author. Here again there is assurance and confidence.

A joy that every Bible student shares is the realization that one theme exists throughout the whole Book. "God so loved the world, that he gave his only begotten Son, that whosoever believeth in him should not perish, but have everlasting life" (John 3:16). Nothing in the Bible will ever contradict that!

One of the heartbreaking experiences in life is the inconsistency of people. One's supposedly best friend can change, thus bringing heartache. What does it mean to the sorrowing, hurting soul of man to learn that the Word of God never changes? What effect could the fact that God's Word is unchanging have on the unsaved man? What effect could the fact that God's Word is unchanging have on the growing Christian? List five ways a person could show that the Bible is unchanging. What conclusion could any logical thinker come to after examining the Bible and seeing its consistency in every aspect even though many sections of it were written hundreds of years apart with none contradicting the other? What has this lesson taught you personally about the Bible?

7. It Is Everlasting
I Peter 1:25

This is a passing world. Only the things of God are everlasting or eternal. The sentence of death is upon everything in this world! Every flower must die. The grass will wither—but the Word of the Lord endures forever (I Peter 1:25).

The only thing in this world that is guaranteed never to be destroyed or changed is the Word of God. When I hold the Bible in my hand I hold something that will never be done away.

Institutions will crumble, traditions will fade, customs will change, but the Bible will never be altered.

This is a great comfort to the heart. Regardless of the changes in the affairs of men, and no matter how many wonderful things become obsolete, the Bible will always bring the same comfort, the same assurance. No matter how many new items may be invented by man it will always be true that "in the beginning God created the heaven and the earth."

And it is a great assurance to the mind of man; no matter how often and how much men may change what they say and do, there is an underlying permanence in the arrangement of things. All natural processes continue as they have—and will.

Thus it is with the Bible. Just as Christ on Calvary is always and forever the Saviour from sin, so is the open grave and the glory of Pentecost a permanent blessing. And this is what the Bible tells!

List five important things you now have which will some day be gone. If you are a Christian list five things you now have, which you will enjoy forever because you belong to God. What does it mean to you personally that God's Word is eternal? Name several reasons you can use in showing someone that the Bible is "eternal"? Will this lesson cause any changes to be made in your personal life? If so what?

Make a Decision

"I am the Way, the Truth and the Life," said Jesus Christ. That is, Jesus Christ is the last word from God to man. When we see Jesus Christ there just isn't any more to see. When we read through God's Word, the Bible, we can put a period at the end, for that is *it!!*

It should give our hearts joy to think upon the finality of the Bible—to realize that it will *never* be obsolete. It is more up-to-date than tomorrow's newspaper. And it is yours. Are you reading it? How often and how much?

CHAPTER 4

Records Were Kept

Bible reading for this week: II Kings 22:8-14

The people of God have always depended upon God to lead them by revealing His will to them. Sometimes He revealed His Word to chosen men who were sent to tell the message to all.

Since He did not reveal Himself even to His chosen servants every day, and since the events which occurred were not repeated, it was important that records of the revelation should be kept.

Paul said such records were written for our learning. These records were part of the Scriptures. This helps us to realize that the history recorded in the Bible was not written to tell about Israel as a nation, but rather it was written so that we could learn the ways of God and be able to walk in them now.

1. Of the Words of the Law
Deuteronomy 9:10

The law of Moses was based upon Ten Words given on Mount Sinai. During forty days of communion with God Moses received two tablets of stone on which were written by the finger of God the Ten Words we have come to know as the Ten Commandments.

All the circumstances of this event emphasized the unusual importance of this revelation. It was made very clear that what was done was under the control of God Himself. No one has ever offered any explanation of how the words were written on the tables of stone.

It is true that much of what was set forth was already understood as the measure of what was right, but at no time had there ever been any such concise, definitive statement of what God required in His own righteousness. From this time on in the history of God's people, these Ten Words became the basis of any formulation of God's instruction to His people.

Because ot the incident of the golden calf, Moses cast these tablets of stone bearing the Ten Words upon the rocks and shattered them. Such an act was symbolic in a dramatic way of the significance of the idolatrous sin of the people in making and worshiping the golden calf.

After his judgment of the sin of Aaron and of the people, and his wonderful prayer of intercession, (Exodus 32:31,32) Moses again received two tables of stone with the Words of the Covenant. Everything about this event stresses the fact that the author of the Ten Words was God Himself. By having them written on stone the truth of their permanent unchangeable character can be seen.

Why is it customary for men in business to request that the terms of any proposed agreement be "put in writing"? Name at least four agreements in business that are normally put in writing. What difference does it make if a piece of property is "posted"? What is the value of traffic signs? Can a traffic sign guarantee safe driving?

2. Of the Instruction to His People
II Kings 22:13

Guidance from God would come both in matters that pertain to the nature of God and also in matters that were related to the affairs of the people. As pertaining to the nature of God the revelation could be permanent and eternal, and this is to be seen in the Ten Words given to Moses on Mount Sinai. But as related to the affairs of the people the instructions could be specifically designated to meet the needs of that time.

In addition to the Ten Words inscribed on the

tables of stone, there were instructions given to the people of the nation and to their rulers. Even though such guidance would necessarily be limited to that particular situation, it was nonetheless the will of God. Such instruction was never developed in the thinking and the judgment of men, which would have permitted additions or alterations; but it was always given in a final form as authorized by God and inspired by his Holy Spirit.

The permanence of the pronouncements as made was implied in having them written. Their form was not dependent upon the accurate memory of anyone. Their being written allowed no uncertainty as to exactly what the will of God was.

There is an impersonal aspect in the form of the written Word which contributes to impartiality. It remains as it is in any changing future or circumstance—it plays no favorites.

Just as a compass maintains its function regardless of varying conditions of weather, even so the written record of the instructions given by the Lord through his Spirit-led servants remained unaffected by the changing circumstances or leadership of the people.

Why are the "orders of the day" posted on bulletin boards? Why are instructions in printed form enclosed with appliances when they are sold on the open market? Why are directions found on every bottle of medicine? What did Jesus of Nazareth teach about the authority of Old Testament guidance? How did Jesus of Nazareth meet temptation (Matthew 4:3-10)? What did Moses command Israel to do so that they would be aided in keeping the

Law (Deuteronomy 27:1-8)?

3. Of Words Added by the Lord
Jeremiah 36:32

Something very significant happened to the roll of parchment upon which Baruch the Scribe had written the message of instruction to Israel from God which He had made known through the prophet Jeremiah (Jeremiah 36:4 and 23). The fact that the king could order the roll to be burned shows clearly that man may disregard and even discredit the message from God brought to man through a prophet.

The fact that another roll was prepared and that the same message was written therein points to the fact that although rebellious man may hinder proper attention to the Word of God, he cannot really destroy it.

Today there are critics who so handle the text of Scripture that for many people the result is that the written Word is actually destroyed. But God, the Author, has not been changed. His will has not been altered. All the destructive criticism of the text of Scripture does not change the mind of God. And God will arrange to have the same message restated just as it had been first given.

Yet there was a significant addition of "many like words" (Jeremiah 36:32). The king had been especially annoyed because the message announced judgment upon him in his rule. When he caused the written words to be burned he did not in any way affect the will of God about himself. What actually happened was not only that the original message was reaffirmed, but also there was actually more of the same about what would happen to him.

This may well be a warning to Bible critics today; in attempting to discredit the text of the Bible such men may only be increasing the judgment of God upon themselves.

If a man understood he had reached a certain agreement in a business deal, and later it developed that the written contract he signed had provisions in it different from what he understood in his discussion, which conception of the agreement would be valid? Why? If a man agreed to an arrangement and then before it was put into effect, decided he wanted different conditions, what procedure should he follow before he signed? If a man were moved in a church service to respond to the preacher's call to accept Christ, what else should that man do? Why? What procedure should anyone follow before signing the acceptance of any contract? Why?

4. Of the Length of the Captivity
Daniel 9:2

The Bible is the written revelation of the will of God. Sometimes there is revealed some aspect of the eternal plan of God to save by Jesus Christ those who would respond to the call of the gospel and yield themselves unto the will of the living Lord. Sometimes there is revealed some aspect of God's will as pertaining to the particular situation existing at a given time in the history of His people. To serve its full purpose the Scripture needed to be believed by the people of God.

Jesus of Nazareth pointed out that He spoke about temporal things of this world so that people could see for themselves that what He said was true; and that He did this to win their confidence, so they would believe Him when He also spoke about eternal things of the invisible world.

In dealing with Israel in Old Testament times God affected their temporal affairs by His guidance and His help. He brought them out of Egypt, led them across the desert, and brought them into the land of Canaan. All this was openly seen. He watched over Israel as a nation and guided the course of their affairs in open fashion, which could be noted by anyone.

In the course of His guidance it was necessary to chastise the nation by letting an enemy capture Jerusalem, destroy the temple and carry the people into captivity. It would have been easy to interpret all this as natural events and so miss the truth God wanted His people to learn. He wanted them to know that their defeat in war and their loss of blessing was directly a judgment from Him because of their incorrigible disobedience.

So He revealed the length of time their captivity would last. He moved Jeremiah to write down in His book that Judah would be held in captivity for 70 years. When Daniel read this prophecy He prayed with confidence that Judah should now be released from captivity since the 70 years had been fulfilled. Judah was released from bondage at that very time and was allowed to return to her own land. And the people believed the Word of God.

What impressions was made upon Daniel when he read that the time of the captivity was stated to be seventy years (Daniel 9:2,3)? What does any Bible student think when he reads that the time of the captivity was stated and events proved the prediction to be true? What is taught by the fact that Jeremiah foretold the length of Israel's captivity? Would you say that predicting the time of coming events is necessarily a mark of a real Christian (Acts 1:7)? What definition of a real Christian is indicated in John 20:29?

5. Of the Events in the Life of Jesus of Nazareth
   Luke 1:1

All the faith of a Christian is centered in Jesus Christ. The Christian believes that God is, and that God judges, and that through Christ Jesus he has been reconciled to God and will be pardoned because Christ Jesus died for him as the Lamb of God. The gospel sets forth the truth about Jesus Christ as the plan of salvation. It is when a man accepts this proclamation as true, and commits himself to God on the basis of what Christ Jesus has done, and believes that God raised Him from the dead, that his soul will be saved.

It is essential that the believer should be convinced of the actual reality of the life, death, burial, resurrection and ascension of Jesus of Nazareth. The specific events as they occurred actually matter in the faith of the believer who is being saved. Both to provide a careful, exact report, and to make sure there would be no addition or omission, God in his providence moved men to write down exactly what happened.

Luke tells his friend, Theophilus, this was his purpose in writing his gospel account (Luke 1:1-4). He claims to have had "perfect understanding of all things from the very first," and says that he wrote those things "that thou mightest know the certainty of those things, wherein thou hast been instructed."

John admits that Jesus of Nazareth did many more works of wonder which were not recorded (John 21:25) but these were written so that readers "might believe that Jesus is the Christ, the Son of God" and that in believing they "might have life through his name" (John 20:30,31).

Committing the account of the events of the life of Jesus of Nazareth to writing would give a settled report that would not be subject to change. Since in His Incarnation Jesus of Nazareth lived his life on earth at one point of history and in a certain way, it was entirely proper that the record should be single and settled.

If different persons were writing up the events of the life of Jesus of Nazareth why would Luke take this task in hand (Luke 1:1-4)? Why could anyone want to write such an account? What are the general advantages in having a written record of

what was reported by eyewitnesses of any event?
Why does the patrolman write down all the facts
about a highway collision? How significant is a
diary as evidence in court? What would be some
special reasons for the disciples to write down
things as they happened (II Peter 1:15)?

6. Of the Meaning of the Gospel
II Peter 3:16

The events recorded in the Bible are very important and they should always be taken just as they
were described, without any change by adding or
subtracting anything. But in themselves they are
not enough. It is their meaning that really counts.

When Jesus of Nazareth rose from the dead it
would seem that to show that He was really alive
would be all that would be needed. And He did
take time to show by "many infallible proofs" that
He was actually, literally raised in bodily form. But
this was not His principle concern.

Although Jesus walked with His disciples, ate
with them and opened their eyes to recognize that
He was actually there in person, He also took time
with them to show the real meaning of this event
by opening the Scriptures: "And beginning at
Moses and all the prophets, he expounded unto
them in all the scriptures the things concerning
himself" (Luke 24:27). Nothing in the Scriptures
was needed to establish the fact that He rose from
the dead. He was before them in person. But His

47

bodily presence was not enough to show the *meaning* of the Resurrection. For this the Old Testament Scriptures were needed.

Peter accepted Paul's letters in which he explained the meaning of the gospel, as being "Scriptures" with full authority from God. Peter went on to say that if a man, who was unlearned and unstable twisted those writings, he would do so to his own destruction. Apparently Peter felt that Paul's letters were authoritative interpretations for the instruction of other believers.

What common practice did Peter want to guard against by writing down what had happened (II Peter 3:16-18)? After Jesus was raised from the dead and was present in person talking to his disciples, how did he arrange that they might understand what had happened (Luke 24:27; 45-48)? Besides works of providence, and answer to prayer what is important for understanding and faith (Luke 24:45)? If a person is being shown remarkable events ostensibly by the power of God, for what else should a careful believer ask and look? If a person is hearing a powerful presentation of some idea, and is even fascinated by alleged wonders, what should a Christian ask him to help him believe?

7. Of the Future Plans of God
Revelation 22:18,19

The Bible reveals God's plan for His creation.

The records show what was done in creation and in the affairs of mankind. Then the records show how God's plan for living by faith was promised to Abraham and to his seed, and how events occurred in history as God worked out His will. Then there are records of predictive prophecies that point forward to what God will do as He completes His plan for this world.

Despite the fact that students of such predictions differ in their understanding of when and how fulfillment will take place there is common confidence that such fulfillment will take place, and that it will be found that the predictions will prove to have been true.

The ultimate vindication of the predictions depends upon the occurrence of the actual events predicted and their obvious fulfillment of the predictions. But there is no reason to doubt what is written.

When the prophets wrote of things to come they often did not understand the full meaning of what they were writing (I Peter 1:10-12). When the actual fulfillment of an Old Testament prediction occurred, it was not always easy to recognize it for what it was (Matthew 17:10-13). This should make all students humbly cautious when they propose to identify fulfillments of prophecy.

In the interpretation of visions great care is likewise needed in the matter of identifying the items in the vision. It is possible that all descriptions are symbolic and should not be taken as literal data. Though often vague the details should always be handled as authorized data.

Why is it important that plans for the future be written? What is implied when a man writes down what he is going to do? How is the believer helped when he reads the promises as to what God will do? When is a contract for future services of real value? Describe two contracts in which you are involved, commenting on what they promise. Why is it so important to have the future plans of God set forth in detail for a believer (II Peter 1:4)?

Make a Decision

"No Bible no breakfast" is an old motto many earnest Christians have followed regarding the importance of Bible study in a Christian's daily life. This gives strength for, the comfort for, and help for the unforseen problems which may arise on a given day.

Have you ever tried God's promises for your day-by-day living? Will you try them today? They were written and kept for your learning.

CHAPTER 5
In Everyday Terms

Bible reading for this week: I Corinthians 2:1-5

Faith is the very essence of the life of a Christian. But this means more than a ready willingness to expect things to work out favorably. Faith must have a contact. There must be something that is believed. This is not merely that something was said which is then accepted as having been uttered. It is that the idea expressed is taken to be true. The meaning of the words is received as true.

When the gospel is stated in the vernacular it is both meaningful and effectual. Some may think that the common language of the common people is not adequate to present the gospel, but in actual fact this is the only way in which its communication can be effectual.

1. Using Fables to Show Truth
Judges 9:7-21

Ideas are most clearly recognized when they are acted out in conduct. Gestures and postures convey the deeper meaning of words. Words spoken in prayer are made so much more moving when the head is bowed, the eyes closed, or when the praying person is kneeling.

A similar effect is gained when a story is told that in itself embodies the idea. Actual events in history which illustrate the idea to be communicated are very effective when their story is told. But such events are often not available to serve the need in communication. Sometimes they are too cluttered with other matters that becloud the message intended to be a practical means of getting one point across to the hearers. And yet the story is the most effectual mode of conveying thought.

To meet his need a speaker may create a story, as if it were the narrative of an actual event, which will serve to convey his idea. This is known as a fable. It is not claimed that the event described actually happened, but it is held that the idea illustrated in the story is the truth which the speaker wants to communicate.

The Scriptures include many forms of literary expression, including allegory, such as occurs in Judges 9:7-15. It is there used by Jotham when he gave his answer to the men who asked him to accept his brother Abimelech as king. Jotham no doubt could have answered the suggestion in so many words. He could have said a simple "no." And then he could have expressed his opinion of the whole idea in his own words. But by using the allegory of having trees discuss with each other which of them should be the king over the others, Jotham was able to convey a much richer, more meaningful reply. The use of the allegory challenged the hearer to employ his imagination to see the truth implied and this resulted in a richer, more meaningful communication.

Remembering there were no authorized records of the events in the life of Jesus of Nazareth how would it be possible for allegories to be told about Him? (Luke 1:1). What sort of ideas did His enemies tell about His power to perform miracles? (Matthew 12:24). How did Jesus of Nazareth answer the untrue stories about His work? (Matthew 12:25-29). How did the chief priests and elders arrange to discredit the testimony of the disciples about the resurrection of the body of Jesus of Nazareth? Name two lines of argument Peter proposed to prove that he was not following "cunningly devised fables" when he preached about the incarnation of our Lord Jesus Christ (II Peter 1:16-20).

2. Using Object Lessons to Show Truth
I Samuel 11:7

Every teacher knows the effectiveness of an objective illustration of truth. Children are taught to count by using blocks, pieces of chalk, marbles, and the like. The whole idea of comparison is quickly and clearly conveyed by showing larger and smaller objects together. To tear a written note into shreds is an effective means of conveying the fact that its message has been rejected.

When Saul wanted the tribes of Israel to realize the soberness of his call to them to go to battle under his leadership, he took a yoke of oxen and hewed them into pieces, and then sent these pieces to the several tribes with the warning that such would be the fate of any who failed to respond. The graphic display of the butchered parts conveyed the call much more effectively than mere words could have done.

The Scriptures use obect lessons often to convey truth. The Word of God becoming incarnate is a prime example. Of course, the Incarnation is also much, much more than an object lesson, but let us consider how effectively it conveys truth. When the Word was made flesh, it could be handled and seen. An object is self-evident. The Word of God in bodily form could never be mistaken for opinion, for feeling, or for a mood. When the Word became tangible it allowed no easy dismissal as if it were merely an utterance of an idea.

As an actual body the Word could be sensed as it was. It could not be denied. "Handle me and see!" It could not be changed.

An object is so illuminating with no chance for illusion. There is an integrity about an actual thing. It is honest. It is what it is and it can be so easily remembered as just that.

When the Word of God became written in the Scriptures, and incarnate in Jesus of Nazareth it became an effectual means of communicating the will of God. "He that hath seen me hath seen the Father."

If a man told you he knew of a grocery store where you could buy ripe olives, how could he make his words convincing? If a boy told you his dog was not afraid to chase cattle how could he get you to believe what he said? If a person told you visitors had come from Canada how could this report be established in your mind as true? If a woman claimed that boys had eaten all the cookies in the jar how could she help you to believe it? What would be convincing proof that the gospel can change a man's way of living?

3. Using Practical Proofs to Show Truth
I Samuel 24:11

Man is so often fooled by what he hears, what he thinks he sees, what he imagines, that it is easy for him to doubt the reality of what he has heard. Words alone may not fully convince him. But when practical proofs are actually shown, these generally banish questions in the mind of the hearer.

When David could hold up in his hand the missing part of Saul's blanket, then Saul knew for sure that David had been beside him, close enough to have killed him. In that proof David convinced Saul that he could have killed him, and that he did not want to do so.

When Jesus of Nazareth rose from the dead, the idea of the resurrection of the body was so incredible that the disciples could not and did not believe it to be true. Jesus called upon them to handle him that they might know for sure. The practical proof of His actual body as it was felt by their hands would enable them to believe, to accept as true what was actually, really true! But when He took fish and honey and *ate* before them, doubt was completely pushed aside; the practical proof of the eaten food would forever keep them convinced, that He was really alive!

Even to this day there is no substitute for practical demonstration. It was when the lame man himself stood with the disciples that insinuations as to the claims made by Peter were dropped.

And all this is most valid today. Witnessing is most naturally done by word of mouth, but witnessing must be supported by action on the part of those who really believe.

What is a common procedure for a woman to follow if she wants to know for sure that a piece of cloth is soft? How can a car buyer know whether a certain model handles easily? How could one ever find out whether Bible reading is any help to faith? How could a person ever know for sure whether a promise in Scripture is valid? When a prediction in the Bible is fulfilled, what does that show? Name some predictions about Christ which were fulfilled in the life of Jesus of Nazareth.

4. Using Examples to Show Truth
II Samuel 12:1-14

An example is always helpful in communicating an idea. Words alone are limited by the minds of those who hear. No matter what I mean when I speak, the words I use mean something to the hearer which may be more or less than what I had in mind to say. But when I set forth an example of my idea the hearer can generally know much more clearly what I meant to say.

If Nathan had come to David and told him bluntly he had done wrong, Nathan would have been right and would have told the truth. Yet David might not have recognized just how he was wrong, and could have begun to defend himself in his own mind. But when Nathan told about the shepherd with his one lamb being robbed by a sheep owner that already had many sheep, David could see the wrong clearly and was moved to prompt judgment upon the wickedness of the deed. Having seen this clearly it was not difficult for David to judge himself at once, and to confess his sin to God.

Jesus of Nazareth used this method throughout all His teaching. The examples He used were called parables. They all proceeded along the same pattern. Some situation known to His hearers was taken to present a narrative that illustrated the truth He wanted to teach. When His hearers saw and understood the examples, He opened their understanding to the truths He wanted to communicate.

Give four examples of the truth that if anyone is going to be able to help you, that person must know what to do. Give one example in which you were the loser because you trusted someone who did not know what to do. Describe a situation where a teacher was himself an example in teaching a pupil. Give two examples from the Bible to show that praying makes a difference. What new truth have you learned from this lesson? What has this lesson meant to you personally?

5. Using Calamity to Show Truth
I Kings 13:26

Sometimes the truth to be communicated is not readily seen in general principles. It may be that what is to be learned is some aspect of the mind of God that no man could ever guess with any assurance. It can be the sort of thing you would never believe unless you actually saw it happen. In His providence God can have things happen that will show what is to be learned.

Who would ever believe that God would take the life of a faithful prophet because he allowed himself to be deceived by another prophet? The truth is, God would; and He showed it in the case of the young man of God who came to warn Jeroboam (I Kings 13:26)!

Who would ever believe that God would not allow his faithful servant Moses to enter into the

land of promise because he had sinned, even though
Moses definitely prayed for this? But that is exactly
what the record shows (Numbers 20:7-13; Deuteronomy 3:25-27)! Who would believe that God could
let a man be born blind in order to show what He
could do to help? But this is what happened
(John 9:1-3)!

The Bible teaches that God works all things
together for good to them that love Him. This will
extend even to any calamities that may occur. In
any such case the believer will look to see what
lesson is being set forth "for our learning"!

List a tragic happening in history that clearly set
forth a basic truth. List a tragedy that happened in
your family and point out what truth it showed.
What did Jesus of Nazareth indicate as a lesson
from the tragedies mentioned in Luke 13:1-5. Name
several tragedies reported in the Bible and point
out the truth which was revealed in them. Write
out Romans 8:28. What does this verse mean to you
personally?

6. Using Violence to Show Truth
   II Kings 10:28

The only world we know includes death. As
desirable and as pleasant as life may be, death is
just as real and common. Death has passed upon all
men. It is appointed unto man once to die.

God is Lord of life, but He is also Lord over
death. Just as no man can live by his own strength,

just so no man dies by himself. It is a common error to think that God always helps living, but that death is somehow a condition in which God for some reason could not bring His will to pass. This is very misleading. The truth is that "the Lord giveth, the Lord taketh away."

At certain points we read that God will bring destruction upon the wicked, and somehow we can accept that in the eternal sense, but when destruction actually occurs now in this world among us, we have difficulty accepting the fact that this too is in the hands of God!

Israel had a tendency to forsake God and to worship Baal. Ahab brought his wife Jezebel into Israel from Sidon, and through her Baal worship was brought into Israel. This would bring disaster. Israel must be warned. The people needed to know for sure that God would destroy Baal worshipers.

Jehu was a stern reformer who dealt drastically with Baal worship as a surgeon would deal with gangrene or with a malignant tumor. It is shocking to read of his violent methods, but the record shows that Baal worship was thus destroyed (II Kings 10:28).

The Bible records violent treatment of sin that we might learn the sinfulness of sin and the judgment of God upon sin!

What can one learn from "the soul that sinneth it shall die"? What truth was shown when the man who blasphemed was put to death (Leviticus 24:13-23)? What is to be learned from the death of Nadab and Abihu in Leviticus 10:1-11? What lesson was taught when Miriam was stricken with leprosy

(Numbers 12:9-15)? Why was the Sabbath breaker put to death (Numbers 15:32-36)? What did the judgment upon Korah teach (Numbers 16:1-40)?

7. Using Plain Talk to Show Truth
Nehemiah 8:8

The Word of God must be understood. Just because eternal things are invisible, and because the will of God cannot be imagined by any human heart or mind, it is necessary that He reveal His will to us. And this He has done.

"Eye hath not seen, nor ear heard, neither have entered into the heart of man, the things which God hath prepared for them that love him. But God hath revealed them unto us by his Spirit" (I Corinthians 2:9,10). Because this is true the Christian should read and study the Bible eagerly to discover what God has prepared for him. He needs to *understand* what has been written so that he may *know* for his own benefit.

Nowhere in the Bible is there any suggestion that merely reading the words or hearing their sound as uttered has any magic effect. But there is clear indication that it is extremely important that believers understand the meaning of what is written.

When the Jews returned to their land to rebuild Jerusalem and to restore their own way of living, Ezra took special steps to insure that the people would know by understanding what God had given them to know. He opened the book and read "in the

61

law of God distinctly, and gave the sense, and caused them to understand the reading." This was making sure that the people had plain talk about Bible truth for everyday living.

Long afterwards Paul emphasized the importance of understanding the Scriptures and of worshiping in an understanding way (I Corinthians 14:15-19).

List five important truths which are stated in the Bible in plain words. What is the plainest warning you were ever given? What was the plainest guidance you ever received? When did you ever make a mistake because the instructions were not clear? What does Paul say about the importance of speaking plainly in public worship (I Corinthians 14:4-19)? What new truth have you learned from this lesson? How has this lesson affected your personal life?

Make a Decision

"Faith without works is dead," says the apostle James. That is, faith that does not work is not saving faith. In other words faith that saves, works. Not in order to be saved but because the individual is saved.

A believer's works in the Lord are actually the outward signs of what has happened in the heart. We love Him because He first loved us. Is your faith working? Continuously through the day? It is the work of God that you believe on Him whom He has sent.

CHAPTER 6

Seeing Is Believing

Bible reading for this week: II Peter 1:12-18

When the Word was made flesh, and dwelt among us the communication of the truth of God was immeasurably helped. The promises of God need to be believed to become effectual. Hearing them in so many words as uttered in preaching is always essential but this may not in itself be enough. When the truth stated in words can also be seen in actual manifestation, it is easier to have real conviction about it.

This is what Peter had in mind when he recalled how he was affected when he heard the voice from heaven on the Mount of Transfiguration (Matthew 17:5 and II Peter 1:16,17).

1. Looking at the Stars Helped Abraham to Believe
Genesis 15:5

To believe means more than having confidence in the objective accuracy of a statement. It also means having some idea as to the meaning of the statement. "Believing it" means not only accepting it as accurate, but also understanding the meaning to be true. A person needs to know the meaning of the words spoken in order to *believe* them.

When Abraham was told that his seed would be a countless host, he could have some idea of the fact that the multitude would be so large that no one could count them. But when he was taken out and told to look into the sky to see the stars, and then told his seed would be like *that*, he would then be able to believe in a new dimension. When he was taken to the shore that he might see the sands of the sea he would have a much better grasp of the promise concerning his own descendants.

This is a common device in Scripture by way of communicating the meaning of what was expressed in so many words. To show the frailty of human life the Bible says "all flesh is grass" and then goes on to say "the grass withereth," making this meaning much more vividly clear.

Probably no more eloquent expression is possible than to say, "What is your life? It is even a vapour, that appeareth for a little time, and then vanisheth away." By such figures of speech the Bible helps the reader to grasp the meaning that he may believe.

What is the meaning of the Chinese saying "one picture is worth a thousand words"? Give two illustrations of tools that would be hard to describe but which can be understood at once when they are seen? How did Jesus of Nazareth picture: (a) the importance of obeying His words? (b) the importance of being ready for His coming? (c) the importance of being humble when you pray? (d) the importance of giving to the poor? (e) the power of the gospel? (f) the forgiveness of God?

2. Miracles Helped Moses to Believe
Exodus 4:1-9

The gospel is based upon the wonder-working power of God. Salvation is the work of God in which He exercised His power to do His will in overruling the processes of nature in this world. In the saving of a soul God performs a new creation which is just as real and actual as the first creation. The new creation is different in its essence as indicated by saying it is spirit as contrasted with the first creation which is called flesh. The promises of God, which are yea and amen in Christ Jesus, involve the creative power of God whereby He replaces the processes of natural flesh by instituting the processes of the Spirit.

To believe this Moses needed to be confident that God could set aside natural processes at will. When God turned his rod into a serpent and then back into a rod again, Moses had concrete evidence. In the same way when his hand was made leprous and then again made whole before his very eyes Moses was helped to believe in the power of God as being able to carry out His promises.

In all the wonders which were done in the plagues which came upon Egypt, Moses participated with assurance. He could announce to Pharaoh what would happen at his word, with an impressive confidence which finally convinced Pharaoh that it would be well to grant the request to let his people go. Such confidence was not simply a matter of logical conclusion based upon rational considerations, but was directly the result of manifestations of power shown to Moses in miracles.

Name several promises in the gospel which involve acts of God which are like miracles. Name several miracles in Old Testament history and point out how they can affect a person's faith. Name several miracles performed by Jesus Christ and point out how they affected faith. Write out II Corinthians 5:17. What does this verse mean to you? How would you explain the new birth to a seeking soul?

3. The Tabernacle Helped Israel to Believe
Hebrews 8:5

One aspect of tne gospel sets out the conditions on which a sinner can come into the presence of God to worship Him. While it is wonderfully true that anybody can come to God, it is not true that one can come in any way he chooses. God is holy and of purer eyes than to behold sin. A sinner in his sin cannot stand before God.

God in His grace provided the means by which a sinner can come to God. Certain things must be done and these things must be taken by faith by the worshiper to be his own. Since they are so directly involved in the very nature of God they could never be known, or even anticipated, in the mind of man.

These things have an intrinsic relation to one another, and to know about them one must know this relationship.

All this has been graciously revealed in the tabernacle. Moses was shown this pattern on the mount when he received the tables of stone, and this structure of relationships among the various things involved was set forth first in the design of the tabernacle and afterward more permanently in the temple.

The furniture of the tabernacle in the exact arrangement as prescribed shows the truth of God's will about sinners, who come to worship. Such a worshiper must come to the altar to confess his sin. Then he must submit to the washing at the laver. After that he can understand by the candlelight and be nourished by the shewbread. Finally he comes to the altar of incense that he might praise God and give thanks for blessings received.

Once Israel understood this she could believe with confidence.

What benefits will follow from having a separate church building in which to worship God? Do you think the architecture of a church building contributes to the meaning of worship? What advantage would there be in having a formal "order of worship" to follow in a service? What difference if any do you see between having a pulpit in the center of the rostrum and having the communion table in the center? Why might the rule of a church require that the Scriptures should be read during any and every service? What significance can you see in having the choir singers wear gowns?

4. Ceremonial Regulations Helped Israel to Believe
Leviticus 11:44-47

Some of the truth of the gospel applies to the conduct of the believers. When it comes to the matter of receiving blessing from God, it makes a difference how a person lives. Even though a person may be reconciled to God because of the offering of a substitutionary sacrifice, it will still be necessary to live in obedience to the will of God if he is to receive blessing.

Since God willed to live in the midst of His people they needed to know that their conduct in every daily matter was a matter of importance to God. Since the natural ideas of the natural man often permit actions that involve sinful elements, the Word of God as revealed through His servants gave specific instructions about personal conduct.

The whole concept of clean and unclean was set forth in many specific regulations concerning foods, clothing, personal conduct, and the like, which emphasized the truth that every detail of conduct mattered to God. The basic truth is that some things are acceptable to God and some things are not acceptable to God. Some things will do and some things won't do. It is just as simple as that.

The fact that these regulations applied to daily activities would convey the truth of clean and unclean into the consciousness of the people. Such insight would affect the whole outlook of a believer and become a definite part of his understanding of the gospel.

Can you see any basic value for a marriage in performing it by means of a church wedding ceremony? Why would the regulations of a denomination outline the ceremony for a person joining the church? What is the importance of a standard procedure for the Lord's Supper? Why does the church outline the questions to be asked in the ceremony of baptism? What is the significance of having a man kneel while he is being ordained as a minister?

5. The Fleece Helped Gideon to Believe
Judges 6:36-40

Sometimes a believer is in a critical situation and finds it hard to be sure that he knows what the will of God really is at that juncture. It would be so easy to fall into wishful thinking. He may read the Scripture and see the promise of God clearly in plain words, yet feel uncertain that he should actually take this to be true for himself. In such a case it often happens that the believer will ask for some sign or omen that will assure him he is really in God's will.

Gideon had been led to the point where a major victory could be his. God had guided and had blessed him till now. He had reason to believe the course of action before him was the will of God, even though its success would be a major wonder to all. He had no reason to doubt, and yet he was fearful of being mistaken because so much was at stake. He felt he needed some sign that God would really be with him and bless him.

Gideon did not doubt the power of God. There is no indication that he doubted the will of God to bless him and His people through him. But he seems to become unsure of his own understanding of God's will. He could do his part only if he believed in God and in God's promise at this specific time. So he planned a testing situation in which God could show him beyond any reasonable doubt that He would actually bless him.

Gideon's fleece has become known as a classic example of being reassured of the will of God to help and to bless. While we do not use fleece today in this way, seeking assurance is always healthy, and the believer can expect that God will satisfy him in any sincere desire to find assurance.

Why did Gideon think what happened to the fleece was not just coincidence (Judges 6:36-40)? What might encourage Christians to operate a city mission for preaching to strangers? Considering the opposition and the cost, why do churches send missionaries to foreign countries? Why should anyone think the translation of the Bible into a tribal dialect will be of any help? What does Acts 16:6-10 mean to you personally?

6. Miracles Done By Jesus of Nazareth Encouraged Belief
John 2:11

The promises of God are revealed in His Word. When that Word is spoken the promise is often stated in so many words, and then commended by some form of reassurance or argument. Much can be communicated in this way. Yet often words alone fall short of convincing power. The hearer may be aware of the chance that something is being misunderstood, mistaken or overstated. Any statement will be more convincing if there is some actual event that demonstrates what has been said.

Jesus of Nazareth offered Himself as the Son of God. Even if He had been known for honesty and His integrity were unquestioned, it would be hard for the folks who grew up with Him and who knew His relatives to believe that He was the only begotten Son of God. Those who heard the voice from heaven on the day of his baptism could have been impressed by that in a special way. But when He performed miracles it was easier to believe in Him.

Nicodemus had admitted that Jesus' miracles were the evidence that He was from God (John 3:2). When He turned the water into wine, "His disciples believed on him" (John 2:11). And so it was throughout his ministry (John 11:45).

This presents a principle for trusting the Bible to be the Word of God. The very fact that it produces results in lives and in circumstances being changed for the better, is evidence that God is in it, doing His work (Acts 5:38,39).

Why are personal testimonies given during an evangelistic service? Alcoholics Anonymous plans regular times for personal testimony of victory. Can you suggest why? Why do testimonies of answers to prayer help in encouraging others to pray? Name three examples of using personal testimony in salesmanship. What use is made of this principle by famous athletes? Tell of one experience in your own life where you accepted or did something because of someone else's testimony?

7. Exposition of Old Testament Scripture Enabled the Ethiopian to Believe
Acts 8:35-37

The gospel comes to men as a message of promise from God, who created everything. It is claimed that the salvation promised in the gospel is the eternal plan of God, and that He had it in mind before the foundation of the world. This fits in with the idea that God is eternal and that believers are His own forever.

Because of this there is a fitness about the Old Testament Scriptures being used to help men understand and to believe the authority of the promises in Jesus Christ.

When Jesus of Nazareth was raised from the dead and wanted the disciples to appreciate what had happened so that they could share in all that was now made available in Him and through him, He not only came to them in person that He might show by many infallible proofs that He was really alive; but he opened their understanding that they might understand the Scriptures (Luke 24:44,45).

We can see an illustration of this in the case of Philip and the Ethiopian (Acts 8:26-40). The Ethiopian had been reading Isaiah but he had not come to saving faith in Christ. When Philip expounded the Scriptures, the Ethiopian was able to believe at once.

Here again we glimpse a very real mission of the Scriptures of both the Old and New Testaments. The Old Testament will state the promise, whereas the New Testament in explaining it will enable one to believe.

How does the story of creation in Genesis help a person to understand the promise of being saved by Christ? What light does knowledge of the Fall cast upon contemporary society? What truth does the flood teach? What lessons can be learned from the story of Joseph? What does the Passover at the time of Moses show about the gospel? What can be learned from the victory of David over Goliath? What does all this show about the study of the Old Testament?

Make a Decision

God works in wondrous ways to enable the sincere soul to trust Him fully. He may use a Scripture verse, the life of a Bible character, or some believer's personal testimony of his walk with the Lord.

This is one reason why it is so important that the believer bear witness to the hope that is within him. Have you ever spoken *one word* for your Lord? Are you going to? Today? Tomorrow? The night cometh when no man can work. Now is the acceptable time. Now is the day of salvation.

CHAPTER 7

Every Man for Himself

ı

Bible reading for this week: John 3:16

The gospel involves the individual believer with God through the Lord Jesus Christ. A common mistake is to talk about the church and the Lord as if that were the basic relationship. The truth is that Christ Jesus deals with sinners one by one.

This can be seen in the Lord's Supper. The bread is eaten and swallowed by each believer, even though in concert with other believers. Again, it is the individual person who takes the cup in his hand to drink it.

The New Testament does not primarily use collective nouns. There is no reference to homes, but there is mention of husbands, wives, children and servants. Primacy of attention is given to governors and citizens rather than to the communities they comprise.

1. Abraham
Genesis 12:1-3

The Tower of Babel was a group project and is a classic example of the work of man (Genesis 11:3,4). What happened to that project in the judgment of God would seem to indicate that such efforts will never succeed in their purpose (Genesis 11:7). Certainly in all the history of the world men have never been able to achieve lasting community in any enterprise (see Acts 5:38).

The call of Abraham is a classic example of the work of God. Not only was the call personal and individual, but the guidance given led Abraham to separate himself from others that he might walk alone with God. He was called out of his land which meant separation from his culture. He was called out from his kindred. He was led to separate from Lot, his nephew, and afterward from Ishmael, his own flesh. In fact he was even called to separate himself from his own future when he was led to offer up Isaac.

And yet even in the covenant with Abraham, made alone with him, the whole world is involved. In his seed all the nations of the world will be blessed. Apparently God deals with the one man and through him deals with all men. Paul stresses the fact that the promise was made to the seed of

Abraham (Galatians 3:16).

What was the religious faith of Abraham's father? List the events as they occurred which brought Abraham away from other people. How did Abraham show that he did not want any human being to receive praise for making him rich? How did Abraham show his godly righteousness in dealing with Lot (Genesis 13:8,9;14:13-16)? How did Abraham show his meekness in dealing with Ishmael (Genesis 21:9-14)? How did Abraham show his faith in God in the matter of Isaac (Genesis 22:2,10-12)? What has this lesson taught you about trusting God?

2. Moses
Exodus 3:5

The deliverance of the children of Israel involved large numbers of people but it was effected by God's working in and through one man—Moses. Oppression of the Hebrews by the Egyptians was common to all the people but did not come upon Moses who was being brought up in Pharaoh's household. The decision that he would not be called the son of Pharaoh's daughter was his own (Hebrews 11:24-26). The killing of the Egyptian taskmaster who was abusing the Hebrew workman was the act of Moses himself.

When God called Moses through the burning bush (Exodus 3:4-6), he was coming to do something that would affect all the children of Israel, but Moses was alone before God when he was called. Moses insisted upon having someone to help him and God appointed Aaron to this role, but the mission to serve God by leading His people out of Egypt remained the personal responsibility of Moses.

Despite the fact that the fortune and welfare of all Israel was the real purpose of the Exodus, the whole movement developed and occurred as the direct consequence of what happened through Moses. It was Moses alone who confronted Pharaoh. It was at the word of Moses that one plague after another came upon all Egypt. It was Moses who would pray to God that a particular plague should be stayed.

Yet Moses himself was not the real reason for all that was happening to him. Looking at Moses helps the reader to realize that this is the pattern of all that happens in the life of faith. The believer is blessed from God in his own personal affairs, but above and beyond this is the consequence that through him others will be helped.

How did Moses' parents show their faith in God (Hebrews 11:23)? How did Moses show his faith in God as a young man (Hebrews 11:24-26)? How had Joseph arranged to keep the promise of the land of Canaan in the minds of the Hebrews (Genesis 50:24-26 and Hebrews 11:22)? How did Moses learn that the deliverance of the children of Israel would not be by what he personally could or would do (Exodus 2:11-15)? What evidence is there that even at eighty years of age Moses still thought the deliverance would have to be by something he personally did (Exodus 3:11; 4:10)?

3. Joshua
Joshua 1:9

Joshua followed in the footsteps of Moses and is another demonstration of the truth that God deals with each man personally and individually. As God dealt with Moses so he dealt with Joshua, and this points to a truth in every case of faith. God has all men in mind when he deals with the individual, but the experience of each man is peculiarly his own.

Joshua was treated differently after the responsibility of leadership came upon him. He is mentioned earlier in the record and was the outstanding military leader during the march across the desert (Exodus 17:9-13). But when Moses was dead and Joshua was to be the leader in his place (Joshua 1:16-18), God treated Joshua in the special way he had blessed Moses (Joshua 3:7).

From this it can be seen that while God deals with each man individually in his own unique experience, what God does to a man will be related to what that man is to do for others. God had in mind all Israel and through them the whole world when he was blessing and leading Joshua.

In one special spiritual experience (Joshua 5:13-15) Joshua was shown clearly that though he was the top leader of the people of Israel in a human way, he was not actually the one who really had the authority.

This presents a profound truth to the believer. God will deal with each believer in a special way, and will commit a certain task to the responsibility of that believer. Yet the believer is not really in charge. It is for him to be obedient to the Lord even as he serves.

What great lessons did Joshua learn in the battle with Amalek (Exodus 17:8-13)? What did Joshua learn when he was with Moses on the mount (Exodus 24:13; 32:17; 33:11)? What did Joshua learn when he went into the Promised Land as one of the spies (Numbers 13:16)? Why was Joshua confident the children of Israel could enter into the land despite the hindrances (Numbers 14:6-9)? What would it mean to Joshua that he would be spared to enter the land (Numbers 14:30,38)? What gave Joshua the courage to take up the mission of Moses (Numbers 27:18-23)?

4. Gideon
Judges 6:16

Gideon was surprised when he received his call to serve by leading his people out of their bondage. He was humble in his esteem of himself.

Because he was not from a prominent family and was not important in his own eyes he was startled to find that he was being chosen to lead Israel against the Midianites. But he is an example of how God deals with each believer.

Even though a man may realize truthfully that he

has no particular gifts for the call of God, this is no reason to think he will be passed over. Zacchaeus had no idea that he might attract the attention of Jesus of Nazareth when he climbed up the sycamore tree to see Jesus. But the Lord called to him personally and went with him to his house. The call of God will come to any man as he is. God is no respecter of persons.

Because Gideon had been personally in touch with God and received His guidance for conduct from Him, he feared no man. Destroying the idol on his father's farm was a bold deed, but Gideon was strong in confidence because he knew he had been chosen of God to do this very thing. Sending home all but 300 of his troops was a daring thing to do, but he knew this was the clear guidance given to him from God.

The believer in the gospel may be very conscious of his own weakness and unworthiness, and yet be really bold in his witness because he knows he has been sent by his Lord.

Why did Gideon have confidence to accept the idea that he was called of God (Judges 6:11,12,14, 16,22-24)? How did Gideon know what to do (Judges 6:25-27)? Why did the Lord require that many of Gideon's soldiers be sent home (Judges 7:2)? How was Gideon helped to be even more confident in his attack upon the host of Midian (Judges 7:15)? What lessons about faith can be learned from this record involving Gideon? Tell about one experience in your own life where the Lord showed His will for you in an unusual way.

5. David

I Samuel 16:13

The anointing of David to become King of Israel was a surprise to everyone. When his father Jesse brought his sons before Samuel for the selection of the one to be King, David was not even brought in with the others. When he took food to his brothers in the army camp David was not welcome to join in the conversation of the soldiers because he did not rate as one of them. Yet Samuel was led to anoint him even as a lad to become the king of the nation.

When Goliath issued his defiant challenge to the army of Israel, David felt in himself that he should accept that challenge. No one could think one so young could venture to face such an opponent.

It would be a mistake to think David faced him in his own courage or in confidence based upon his own ability or strength. David had the promise of God that he would be helped and he believed God in his own personal affairs (I Samuel 17:45-47). In all his national and international relationships as King, David remained aware of the will of the living God. Even in his sin, David was responsible to God. When confronted by Nathan, he confessed his sin (II Samuel 12:7,13). When his son was stricken ill, David prayed to God. When his son died, he accepted this from God.

David is a classic example of a believer who trusts in God regardless of what others may think as to the wisdom of such a course. When a soul knows that God has called him to accept His grace and believe in the Word of God, he can be strengthened to do the will of God in complete confidence.

When David was ready to take up the challenge of Goliath, whence was the source of his courage (I Samuel 17:26)? When David argued that he should be allowed to face Goliath because of victories he had already achieved while herding sheep, what did he offer as the basis of his confidence (I Samuel 17:37)? How did David show his confidence as he met Goliath (I Samuel 17:48)? In seeing David in Saul's household after his victory over Goliath, what lessons can be learned for a man who wants to live by faith (I Samuel 18:5-14)? Why did David spare Saul when he had opportunity to kill him (I Samuel 24:10)?

6. Daniel

Daniel 6:22

Daniel is a classic example in literature of a courageous young man who stood firm and unshaken in the face of total opposition. In part of his career he was accompanied by three other Hebrew children, but in the greater portion of his life he stood alone.

When he was a student engaged in special study he deliberately sought permission to act differently from others, because he was a believer in God while others were not. Later when facing opportunity to demonstrate the power of God he accepted the challenge of the king to serve him (Daniel 2:16), knowing that his very life depended upon his being helped by the blessing of God.

When he was made the victim of clever connivance so that he was obliged to disobey a court order and so endanger his life (Daniel 6:16), Daniel submitted without protest, having complete confidence in God who could watch over him and would take care of him.

Daniel is an example of the believer who accepts the will of God for himself regardless of what others may do, and who is in perfect peace because he is trusting everything to God. Though the Scriptures report just one such case, the principle revealed here works with any believer. Any Christian can expect God to take care of him according to His promises. If he will so trust God he will bear witness before others to the glory of God.

In what way did Daniel set an example for any young believer who has opportunity to gain personal advantage (Daniel 1:8)? What lessons can be learned from Daniel's behavior in the situation where he had been placed (Daniel 1:8-21)? How did Daniel seize an opportunity to show how God could bless him (Daniel 2:14-16)? Why was Daniel so confident he could meet the challenge (Daniel 2:17,18)? What does Daniel's action in getting appointments for his three companions teach about the life of faith (Daniel 2:48,49)? What does Daniel's experience in being thrown into the lions den teach about the life of faith (Daniel 6:4-28)?

7. Paul

Acts 9:4-6

The life of Paul was spent so largely with others that we can scarcely imagine his ever having any privacy. He was always moving among people. Yet we do know that in a very real sense Paul had dealings with the Lord that were altogether his own in secret.

Others were with Paul on the road to Damascus but in his dealings there with the Lord no one else was included. "What wilt thou have me to do?" was entirely singular.

Later when writing to the Galatians Paul emphasized he received nothing from any human source, only from the Lord (Galatians 1:12).

In Paul's case, he knew what it was to have men forsake him, but he rejoiced to bear witness that the Lord always stood by him (II Timothy 4:16-18).

In his letters to the churches it is evident that Paul had supporters and co-workers, but at the same time his whole confidence was grounded in the personal presence and help of the living Lord.

Paul will always be the prime example of a believer, who is living his life in the will of his Lord. Paul sought to please God rather than men (I Thessalonians 2:4-6). He made it the one purpose of his life to enter into the life that was made possible in Christ (Philippians 3:7-14).

Paul's closest dealings were with the Lord. In this he is the prime example of what is possible for every man who believes.

What aspects of Paul's childhood could have helped him to know about God (Philippians 3:5,6)? What was Paul's early life like in matters of religion (Galatians 1:13,14)? What impression may have been made on the young Saul at the death of Stephen (Acts 6:15; 7:2—8:1)? How was the friendship of Barnabas used in Paul's life (Acts 9:27; 11:25,26)? How did Paul show his humility among the disciples (Acts 19:30,31)? How did Paul show his meekness before the Jews (Acts 21:26)? Write out Galatians 2:20. What does this verse mean to you personally? What more should it mean?

Make a Decision

Salvation is the work of God in one soul. He will come into that soul and make his abode there. He will then guide, comfort and keep that soul day in and day out.

Salvation means more than being saved from hell. Thank the Lord you are not going to hell, but you are going to heaven!! But remember that heaven begins here and now when you receive Jesus Christ into your soul. It has been said "If you don't have any heaven in your soul here and now you certainly won't be there later." How is it with your soul? Is all well with your soul? Are you living in the consciousness of Christ's indwelling presence? What else is more important to you than this? What changes are you prepared to make to bring your life to the place you know it should be?

CHAPTER 8

In Every Way

Bible reading for this week: John 20:30,31

The gospel comes to the sinner as a revelation from God. It presents a promise of eternal life to anybody who accepts and believes in Jesus Christ, as He is presented in the Scriptures of the Old Testament and the New Testament.

To be able to receive Jesus Christ for what he offers Himself to be and to do, the soul must hear and understand the revelation set forth in the Bible. In order that anyone may hear and understand the revelation, it must be communicated effectually to the consciousness of the hearer. A simple record in so many words may be neither impressive nor convincing. The language of communication used in various classic styles can be more effective.

1. By Song
Luke 1:46-55

The song is effectual because it is pleasing to the hearer. Since the melody is a pleasure to hear, it can be repeated again and again without becoming tiresome. The same words which express some basic idea can be repeated in the refrain after each stanza, and so make a deeper and more lasting impression. Stanza after stanza setting forth aspects of the truth will be listened to as if they were already partly known because the melody is the same. Thus the ears will hear the message because the tune is agreeable.

The delight in the hearing of music will encourage repetition of the song, and thus the form of the message can be registered in the memory simply as a result of being heard over and over. Songs are usually written in poetic style with rhythm in accent upon syllables and sometimes with rhyme which ties lines together in a natural tonal pattern. Choice of words and the poetic turning of phrases with poetic license in allusions and suggestions, aid even more to make the singing and the hearing of the song a desirable experience, so that repetition will be welcomed with interest and anticipation.

Paul instructed Christians to promote their own spiritual experience by "speaking to yourselves in psalms and hymns and spiritual songs, singing and making melody in your heart to the Lord" (Ephesians 5:19; Colossians 3:16). The repetition of basic ideas in a pleasing refrain would store the memory

with ideas that would be useful in growing understanding of the truth of the gospel.

Name your three favorite hymns. What do you
remember most clearly about any song? Why does
a song have a chorus? Why do radio and television
commercials often sing their announcements? What
sort of personal experience is conducive to the
inspiration of Negro spirituals? National anthems?
Rock and roll? Psalms and hymns? Record here an
experience in which a hymn had a special blessing
for you?

2. By Commandments
Exodus 20:1-17

The law of God is what it is because of the
character of God. God is as He is in Himself and is
unchangeable. This means that what He approves
and what He disapproves will never vary. Change
may occur in the ideas and the preferences of men,
but there is no such change in God.

Because He is God, whatever He wants is final
without apology or explanation. This makes possible simple statements as to what is required. Since
they are authoritative they sound natural when they
are short, absolute directives that simply point out
what is or what is not acceptable.

Obedience is not a logical conclusion which involves an argument, nor is it a conditional action to
be taken when certain prerequisites have been met;
therefore direction can be simply pointed out with-

out preamble or argument. This truth is actually implied when the guidance is indicated in few direct words.

"Trust in the Lord and do good" says it all in so many words. "Cast your burden on the Lord." Following commandments, there are often promises which can comfort the obedient, but these do not vary or modify the simple directive. "Come unto me, all ye that labor and are heavy laden" is followed by a comforting promise, but there is no bearing in that promise upon the commandment itself.

To convey the truth that God is on the throne, the short simple style of the direct commandment is most useful.

Name five well-known signs used to guide the public. What is characteristic of all public directions? When does a posted sign have no meaning for you? Give two illustrations. When are printed instructions hard to follow? Why are highway signs useful? When are traffic signs of no help? Why are there rules? When could a rule, if followed, actually save a life?

3. By Philosophy
Job 32:6-22

The gospel comes to man as a revelation of God's will for man. To be effectual it must be believed. In order to be able to believe the promises, a man must have confidence in the truth of what he hears claimed as the Word of God. Since God is wise, and in His integrity He is consistent and reasonable, the Word of God should be reasonable and should make sense when it is examined in a logical way.

When a message claims to be a revelation from God, it should be possible by analyzing it to see that it fits in with what is already known about God. If it does, it is much more readily received as the truth.

Such study is called philosophy. This can best be recognized as an attempt to *understand*. In trying to understand, a person begins with some ideas and convictions known by direct, original observation. By reasoning he seeks to account for the matter being observed and studied by showing that this is consistent with what is already given and known.

The natural creation shows the power of God. The fitting together of so many natural events shows the wisdom of God. The goodness of providence shows the mercy of God. These and many other like ideas were known by Job. When he considered his suffering in the light of his own conscience and his having diligently and humbly sought to know and to obey God, he was troubled because he could not understand any reason for what was happening to him.

"Come now, and let us reason together, saith the Lord . . ." (Isaiah 1:18). "Consider what I say; and the Lord give thee understanding in all things" (II Timothy 2:7).

Why does anybody offer an explanation when he has done something wrong? If an unidentified noise is heard, what is the first thing any person

91

will do? What is theology? How is it properly distinguished from philosophy? How did Jesus of Nazareth help the disciples understand about His resurrection? What was Paul trying to do on Mars Hill in Athens (Acts 17:16-34)? What do you think about the claim that it is useless to argue religion?

4. By Proverbs
Proverbs 25:1

The Scriptures bring the gospel to man in the common language of the common people. Often people are offended because the truth is put so simply that it is plain to anyone who reads it. This gives no special recognition to the learned or the sophisticated. Everything is written for the wayfaring man. "Thou hast hid these things from the wise and prudent, and hast revealed them unto babes" (Matthew 11:25). No wonder the common people heard Him gladly.

But this simple language can be very profound. Written in words and phrases that are simple, the thought expressed can be very penetrating and illuminating. This can be especially true about proverbs. In concise, clear statements profound insights are made available to enable the reader to understand much more than he could ever express in his own words.

A college student protested in an English course that time spent in studying the text of the book of Proverbs was wasted, because the material was so elementary. The professor assigned to this student the task of writing five proverbs of his own for the next class recitation period. The student came to that class and confessed in shamefaced chagrin that he had not been able to compose even one over a whole weekend.

Proverbs are deceptively simple in form but amazingly apt in revealing truth about relationships. There are thirty-one chapters in the book of Proverbs. A practical reading plan would be to assign each to the corresponding day of the month: thus on May 29 read chapter 29. In this way an easy plan to organize reading can help one to keep it up. Such reading of the book of Proverbs from time to time should greatly improve the wisdom of the reader.

What difference do you think there is between a "proverb" and a "folk saying"? Give several examples of common sayings that you feel are not proverbs. Give five proverbs you find helpful in your thinking. Why are proverbs so convenient in communicating ideas? Are proverbs sufficient to communicate the gospel of Christ? Why?

5. By Parables
Matthew 25:1-13

A parable has been described as an earthly story with a heavenly meaning. It is essentially a story told as an illustration of some specific truth. Using natural, earthly situations and principles the story is composed in imagination to set forth the particular lesson to be communicated. The natural elements are simple and obvious so that the spiritual truth may be unmistakable.

Care should be taken in the interpretation of parables that the intended lesson should be recognized as the one message to be gained. The parable of the sower and the seed (Matthew 13:3-9) was told to impart truth about the hearing of the Word of God. Obviously the story uses processes that occur in agriculture, but it would be a mistake to use this parable for instruction in farming. The parable of the net uses principles to be seen in fishing, but the purpose of the parable was not to help fishermen in their trade. The reader must see in the context the spiritual truth being illustrated so that the purpose of the parable to illuminate the understanding may be achieved.

Sometimes the persons included in the parable may seem to be clearly referring to persons in actual life, but the attempt to use the parable as a means to understand the will of God about real persons or actual situations is not authorized. The parable of the unjust judge (Luke 18:1-8) is told to encourage persistent praying to God, but any attempt to identify the unjust judge as God would certainly be a grave mistake.

In emphasizing that a parable is told to convey one truth, and that one truth only, it is commonly said that one should not make a parable "walk on all fours."

Name five parables in the New Testament, each presenting a different line of truth. Why is a parable so illuminating? Can parables alone communicate the gospel? Why? Why is the parable of the laborers in the vineyard hard to receive? How is a parable like a proverb?

6. By Visions
Ezekiel 1:3-28

A vision has been described as a heavenly story with an earthly meaning. In one sense a vision is like a parable since it is an imaginary construction of known elements to communicate a message that is not known. It is different from a parable in the way a dream is different from an actual event. Where the parable achieves its purpose of communication by telling a story that is so natural that anyone can accept it as true, the vision makes an impression upon the seer which suggests principles that would help in understanding a practical problem.

Ezekiel's vision has baffled all attempts to reproduce it by any artistic means and yet it makes a distinct contribution to the solution of the problem confronting Ezekiel. The young prophet was facing cynical unbelief among his people because of their disastrous natural misfortunes. In this vision he could feel that whereas God's ways are inscrutable and past finding out, they nonetheless move under control "everyone straight forward" (see verse 9). Also, over all there is a throne. What more did Israel need to know?

Peter did not understand what he saw while on

the housetop (Acts 10:17-19), but as events followed in his experience he recognized the import of what he had been shown (Acts 10:28). A vision is not to be analyzed like a statement, or described like an event; it should be read and felt. Like a dream a vision may be constantly changing, so that any attempt to picture it produces only a grotesque caricature. But when the heart is aware of the situation for which the vision was given, it helps to communicate the will of God.

What is a dream? How is a dream different from actual experience of the matters seen in the dream? Illustrate. What is a vision? How did Paul's experience on the Damascus road differ from a vision (Acts 9:3-9)? Tell about three visions in the Bible which have greatly affected you. How is a vision like a parable?

7. By Preaching
Acts 17:22-34

"It pleased God by the foolishness of preaching to save them that believe" (I Corinthians 1:21). Preaching not only sets forth the message in words but it communicates meaning through the manner in which the words are spoken. Paul reminded the Thessalonians, "For our gospel came not unto you in word only, but also in power, and in the Holy Ghost, and in much assurance; as ye know what manner of men we were among you for your sake" (I Thessalonians 1:5).

Certainly this is to say that the gospel comes in word *surely* even though *not* in word only. Paul cautioned Titus to preach with "sound speech, that cannot be condemned" (Titus 2:8). He urged Timothy, "Hold fast the form of sound words . . ." (II Timothy 1:13). He was meticulous in his own attention to the very words of Scripture (Galatians 3:16). Apparently the form of Scripture utterance is significant.

But the Word must be preached also in power, or it is not being really preached! It is only being "said," and is actually an offense to God.

To express the Word of God in an uncertain frame of mind is to defeat one's purpose (I Corinthians 14:8).

Preaching must be in the Holy Ghost. The heart of the preacher must be sensitive at the moment to the things of Jesus Christ. He must be led of the Spirit to say what he says, to whom he says it, and how he says it! The preacher is only "put in trust with the gospel" (I Thessalonians 2:4), and is to realize that he has the duty to deliver it intact, as it was shown to him (Romans 1:14; Galatians 1:11,12, 15,16).

Explain the difference between preaching and teaching. Should preaching and teaching be kept separate? Explain why preaching takes place from a pulpit and teaching is ordinarily in a classroom? Explain why preaching takes place a few times in a week whereas teaching goes on day by day for hours each day? What is the popular idea of "preaching"? How do you expect preaching to be done?

97

Make a Decision

The Bible is God's Word from cover to cover. We see in opening its cover that He used different styles of writing to convey his message to man. However, despite the various literary forms used, it contains one single message from beginning to end —that God will save whosoever cometh unto Him, and that this salvation is possible only through Jesus Christ.

Seeing this great unity should convince man that this book is unique and has one Author. Has this study strengthened your confidence in the Bible? What are you going to do about it?

CHAPTER 9

Same Song in Every Verse

Bible reading for this week: Hebrews 13:8

The gospel of Jesus Christ is the one basic revelation presented to the whole world in the Scriptures. This revelation is communicated primarily in the form of a promise. God will do something for man to help him in his need and misery. All that God will do He will accomplish through His Son Jesus Christ.

Man is in trouble and distress. God so loved the world that he gave his only begotten Son to die for the sins of man, that whosoever would receive him as Saviour would not perish but have everlasting life. This salvation does not occur automatically; salvation is by faith.

1. Promise to Adam and Eve
Genesis 3:15

Throughout the Bible there is one general pattern of affairs that is repeated over and over in never-ending variation—yet with astonishing consistency. The first stage is always the need of man. In personal weakness and sinfulness man finds himself in distress facing destruction. The next stage is always the mercy of God (Psalm 103:13,14), who provides a Saviour. Next to be seen is the grace of Jesus Christ (II Corinthians 8:9). And then comes the final phase when the willing heart receives Jesus Christ as Saviour and Lord, and so is saved by the power of God. Circumstances will vary but the course of action is always the same (Hebrews 13:8).

Despite their wonderful circumstances Adam and Eve sinned when they disobeyed God in eating the forbidden fruit because they were tempted to serve themselves. The condemnation from God followed and man faced death and destruction.

But God came to man in his doom and brought the promise of salvation through the seed of the woman (Genesis 3:15). Then God made coats of skins and covered the nakedness of Adam and Eve (Genesis 3:21).

And so the plan of salvation was outlined. In later events the full details can be seen more clearly. The fact that man must believe in order to be saved by the grace of Jesus Christ is not so obvious in the case of Adam and Eve, but it is clearly implied. This is the only way the grace of God can be received. Believing in the promise of God means much more than simply accepting the account of God's redemptive action. There is involved a committal of the person into the will of God which makes the grace of God operative in the soul.

Of what is needed for living, list what was given to Adam and Eve? What was put within Adam's own control? Why did Adam and Eve disobey God? After Adam and Eve had made aprons to cover themselves why did they hide from view? What is the meaning of responsibility? How was the grace of God manifested in this whole event? What was the result of what Adam and Eve did? How has your life been affected by their disobedience?

2. Promise to Noah
Genesis 9:15

Noah represented a whole new beginning for mankind. When God condemned the world that then was and received Noah and his three sons, a new age was definitely begun. While similar to the beginning with Adam, this had some distinct difference. Adam had been created in innocence and had fallen into sin. Noah had lived amidst a sinful people and had obeyed the Word of God to be called out from among them. The pattern of God's salvation was clearly seen.

Surrounded on every side by sin, Noah shared the common hazard of the judgment of God upon sin. The flood was to come upon the whole world. As one of the children of men Noah was also in danger.

But God was merciful. In judgment he remembered mercy for Noah and arranged for his escape from the flood. He gave Noah specific instructions as to how to build the ark that would save him and his household.

When the rains came and the water rose, God brought Noah into the ark. While Noah had obeyed God in preparing the ark, he could do nothing at the time of the flood. God watched over Noah and in due time brought him out on dry land to replenish the earth.

The very flood from which Noah was delivered by the grace of God was the very means by which the sinful world was destroyed. In the very clouds from whence the rains had come, God placed the rainbow as a sign of his promise that he would never again destroy the world by water. Once again it was demonstrated that God would work out his will in grace despite the sinfulness of men.

What would make it hard for Noah to believe there would be a flood? What did the building of the ark reveal about Noah's faith in God? How was Noah's faith more amazing than Adam's faith? List several of the predictions in the Bible which are not popularly believed true today. What are some common attitudes and judgments held by the public today that the Bible condemns as wrong? How do people explain their rejection of what the Bible teaches? Can you see any of these tendencies within your own heart?

3. Promise to Abraham
Genesis 12:1-3

Abraham is commonly called the father of the faithful. In some respects this man's name is the most *widely* honored name among all men. Jesus of Nazareth has beyond doubt the most *highly* honored name—a name above every name. But Abraham is looked to as the father of the three leading monotheistic religions in the world. The Jews call him "Father Abraham." The Christians know they walk in the ways of Abraham when they believe in God. The Mohammedans count him as their father through Ishmael.

In many respects the life of faith of any Christian follows the classic pattern seen in Abraham. His need was the need of all men. They needed security and they wanted satisfaction. What they sought at Babel and failed to get, Abraham was given by God.

The fact that Abraham sensed his need was shown in his willingness to leave his homeland and his kin in search for blessing. That he looked to receive what he needed and wanted from God is shown by his following the guidance of God into a country where he was a stranger.

He was willing to forsake his nephew Lot and to give up the favorable land around Sodom as he was led. Later he gave up his son Ishmael for the same reason. Finally he even gave up his own son Isaac that he might be obedient to God. In all this Abraham entered into the fullness of God's blessing, and was known as the friend of God.

Name any projects popularly endorsed today that resemble the project of the Tower of Babel. Why are people so ready to adopt any plan that calls for corporate action? Why did the project of the Tower of Babel fail? Why did the project of the Tower of Babel commend itself to the men of Babel? What is humbling to man in the covenant with Abraham? Would you say that Abraham disregarded other people when he followed the guidance of God? Why?

4. Promise to Moses
Exodus 3:7,8

Moses was known as the servant of God. Above all others he is the meek, obedient man who was chosen from infancy to receive the favor of God that he might serve him in great things.

Sometimes it seems that God calls men who have been unusual sinners to show his grace and power, but this was not the case with Moses. His parents were believing people (Hebrews 11:23) and Moses himself was a competent, diligent person (Acts 7:22). The truth seems to be that God can use the willing and the obedient to do his will.

But the pattern of the work of God does not change. The work through Moses began with the Hebrews in distress as slaves under harsh taskmasters. Moses needed to learn that in himself he was quite helpless and unable to do what needed to be done (Exodus 2:15).

In time Moses was called to undertake the task of bringing the people out of Egypt, across the desert, into the land of Canaan which God had promised Abraham he would give to his seed. Moses was very conscious of his own unfitness for this task but was finally induced to commit himself to do it.

Even in calling Moses, God showed himself to be gracious in that he patiently satisfied every misgiving Moses had. As Moses proceeded with his service God was with him to guide him, to help him, to open the way before him. The whole Exodus of Israel was one prolonged demonstration of the grace of God, who brought the people out of their bondage, kept them in all their wanderings and eventually brought them into the Promised Land.

Outline the ways in which the providence of God is to be seen in the life of Moses. What lessons can be learned from Moses' first attempt to help the children of Israel (Exodus 2:11-15)? How was Moses made to feel his own personal weakness in this situation? What lessons can be learned from the incident of the burning bush? What are the various ways in which Moses was given to realize that deliverance of the children of Israel would be God's work and not his own? How does this lesson apply to your own work?

5. Promise to Joshua
Joshua 1:9

Joshua followed Moses and was blessed of God

to become tremendously important to the children of Israel, even as Moses had been (Joshua 1:17). While Moses had served as leader of the people, Joshua had been his servant (Joshua 1:1). He had served as a military commander throughout the Exodus (Exodus 17:9), and had been with Moses on Mount Sinai (Exodus 24:13). He was also one of the spies that had been sent into the land from Kadesh-barnea (Numbers 13:16). But none of these deeds was sufficient to make him able to lead the children of Israel in his own strength or wisdom.

When Moses was dead, the Lord at once called Joshua to assume the leadership and gave him gracious promises of support. The completion of the plan which had been followed by Moses, demanded a strong, prominent leader. God promised Joshua full support and blessing to the same extent he had given them to Moses.

As Joshua took over leadership, God's favor gave him prestige and encouragement. Joshua bravely followed the guidance of the Lord and led the people successfully across the Jordan. After attending to the matter of circumcision, Joshua laid seige to the city of Jericho.

Here Joshua had a vision in which he was shown he was not really the leader of the host of Israel. In this vision he was confronted by One who spoke of himself as "captain of the host of the Lord." When Joshua fell on his face to worship him, he was told, "Loose thy shoe from off thy foot; for the place whereon thou standest is holy" (Joshua 5:15). Once again it was kept clearly understood that salvation is the work of God.

What are some of the disadvantages a young man has who steps into a job where the person who has just left has been very successful? What was the formula given to Joshua to guide him in his entering into the land of Canaan (Joshua 1:3)? How does this formula make special demands upon Joshua's courage? As a spiritual principle, what is the promise of this formula to any believer? If any believer follows this principle what results will appear in his life?

6. Promise to David
II Samuel 7:12-16

David was the greatest king Israel ever had, despite the blemish on his record with Uriah the Hittite.

David was a man after God's own heart. His life was lived in humble dependence upon God in whom he believed and whom he served.

David was anointed to be king of Israel when he was just a lad, too young to share in military service. When Samuel came to Jesse with the word from God that one of his sons would be chosen to become king, Jesse did not even bring David before the prophet to be considered. The task of being king, it seemed, was much too demanding to assign it to one so young and so inexperienced.

When Nathan announced to David that God would establish his throne forever through his descendants, David was overwhelmed because of his own insignificance and unworthiness.

David understood very well that such blessing was not based upon himself but was entirely a matter of the grace of God.

After his anointing the first major deed David performed was his killing of Goliath in battle. The confidence David displayed was not self-confidence. He believed God was with him and would bless him. What looked like personal courage was actually faith in God (I Samuel 17:45-48).

Throughout his great career David looked to God for guidance and trusted in God for help.

What evidence shows that David improved his skills while tending sheep? What was it about Goliath that caused David to feel that he should be challenged? How did David show in his conduct that he would not impose upon the providence of God (I Samuel 18:5-16)? What makes the friendship of Jonathan for David such an unselfish attitude? Is there a situation in your life where such an attitude would be particularly applicable? How did David show he was obedient to the will of God while fleeing from Saul? How did David show that ne did not approve Joab killing Abner (II Samuel 3:27-39)?

7. Promise to the Believer in Christ
John 5:24

The gospel offers to all men everywhere the grace of God through Jesus Christ. Over and over again in the Scriptures the same pattern is seen in every saving work of God. Man is so limited in his own weakness and sin that he is quite unable to cope with the situation he is facing. God in mercy gives man the grace to trust in God. As man believes, God works his will to the glory of his name.

What can be seen in one incident after another throughout the Bible is exactly the situation in which the sinner comes to God through Jesus Christ. Weak, helpless and defiled, the sinning soul is truly with no hope and without God in the world. But "the Son of man is come to seek and to save that which was lost" (Luke 19:10). Jesus of Nazareth said of himself, "I am come that they might have life, and that they might have it more abundantly" (John 10:10).

The great invitation goes out to the whole world: "Come unto me, all ye that labor and are heavy laden, and I will give you rest" (Matthew 11:28). The promise is to all men without respect of persons: Whosoever cometh I will in no wise cast out. It is to the glory of His name that He is able also to save them to the uttermost that come unto God by Him, seeing He ever liveth to make intercession for them. And always it is so graciously true that whosoever will may come.

This offer is open to all who have sinned and come short of the glory of God. And it holds for those who trust Him even though they may falter in their obedience. At no time and in no situation is the justifying grace of God ever dependent upon the works of men (Galatians 2:16). Whatever may be the circumstances Christ Jesus is ready to save.

"Behold, I stand at the door, and knock: if any man hear my voice, and open the door, I will come in to him, and will sup with him, and he with me" (Revelation 3:20).

How does the gospel consider every man as he stands before God? Does saying that God is merciful mean that he will overlook sin? What does it mean? Does forgiveness come to any man simply because he believes the history of the life of Jesus? Why? What must a man believe that he might be saved (Romans 10:9)? What more than intellectual assent is involved in saying, "I believe in Jesus Christ"? Have you ever said this? Did you mean it? What difference did it make in your life?

Make a Decision

The gospel of Jesus Christ is to all men. "Whosoever will may come." The plan of God to save man out of his misery and woe and to bring man unto himself into peace and joy is central throughout the Bible.

God has made all the arrangements for saving all who come unto him by Jesus Christ. This is a message of peace and joy for daily living and confident expectation for the future. Do you have this salvation in your life? Do you have this peace and joy?

CHAPTER 10

The Bread of Life

Bible reading for this week: John 6:33-35

The gospel of Jesus Christ offers to any man the grace of God that he might be saved. One truth emphasized over and over in the Bible is that salvation is of God. Man is in a situation where he is doomed in his own weakness and sin. There is no possible way for him to manage to save himself. It would be like a man trying to lift himself by pulling up on his own boot straps. But God offers to save him and will do so in His own grace and strength.

Just as the body receives nourishment that it may grow and serve from the bread it eats, so it is with the believer. By receiving the promise of God in his Word the believer is saved to the glory of God.

1. Manna from Heaven
Exodus 16:15

The gospel of Jesus Christ is a revelation of God's Word showing how God will save any soul that will receive Jesus Christ as Saviour and Lord. Such salvation is the work of God done to and in and for any soul that believes in Christ. No natural man can believe the promises of God in Christ. But it is true that "whosoever believeth in him shall not perish but have everlasting life."

The Word of God is absolutely essential to the man who wants to be saved. "For whosoever shall call upon the name of the Lord shall be saved. How then shall they call on him in whom they have not believed?" (See Romans 10:13,14.) Faith is necessary but it is not natural. No one is born with faith. "Faith cometh by hearing, and hearing by the word of God" (Romans 10:17).

This is the same as saying that food is absolutely essential to the man who wants to go on living in this world. Bread is necessary but it is not part of the human organism. A man must eat food to have the strength to live. Just so, a man must hear the Word of God to have the faith that will enable him to receive the promises of God.

Bread comes from this world of nature and generates physical strength that enables a person to move about and seek benefits from the natural world. The gospel comes from heaven, from the will of God, and generates spiritual strength that enables a person to believe and to seek the benefits presented in the promises of God. That man has both body and soul is reflected in Jesus' statement, "Man shall not live by bread alone, but by every word that proceedeth out of the mouth of God" (Matthew 4:4).

In view of the account as recorded in Exodus, how should we understand the origin of the manna? How did the New Testament writers handle the Old Testament account of the coming of manna (John 6:30,31)? In view of the Old Testament attitude toward the manna what should we think of the opinion of those scholars who seek a natural origin for this food? What evidence was there that the coming of the manna was an act of God? Why do you think it was necessary to gather it in the morning everyday before the sun was up? Why were the people not allowed to gather it on the Sabbath day?

2. Bread to Eat
Nehemiah 9:15

Man lives in this world by taking food out of his environment and taking it into his body where it is digested, enabling him to grow and to do his work. This means that he is dependent upon his environment for his very life. The air he breathes, the water he drinks and the food he eats come from outside himself. Without air he would smother; without water he would die of thirst; and without food he would starve to death. He is able to live because the world around him is here for his use.

The soul of man lives in the will of God by taking the Word of God from heaven into his own heart and mind, where it is believed and becomes the strength that enables him to obey God.

This means that spiritually he is dependent upon the will of God for his eternal life. The truth he understands, the promises he believes, the commandments he obeys come from outside himself. Without a knowledge of the truth he would be in darkness, without promises from God he would have no hope, and without guidance from God he would be lost. He is able to live spiritually because God gives him grace through his Word.

Man is totally dependent upon God. His life is not his own because it was given to him for his use as a steward of God. His strength is not his own since it is nourished by the food which was given to him. His faith is not his own since that also is a gift from God. His hope is not his own since he must depend entirely upon God for everything in the future.

The truth is that man should humbly yield himself into the will of God inasmuch as everything he has belongs to God and was received from Him. A man should thus be thankful in all things.

How important is bread in a man's life? What are some of the effects of hunger? What is the relation of food to health and strength? In what ways are the Scriptures like the manna? How do the instructions for gathering the manna suggest procedures for Bible reading and study? Have you been following such procedures?

3. Eating the Word of God
Ezekiel 2:9; 3:3

The Word of God brings the revelation of God's will for salvation, but also for service. Hearing the Word and receiving it as a directive is the origin and source of faith. This can be related to the reconciliation of the sinner to God, but it can also be related to the mission to which the believer can be assigned. When a man is estranged from God the Word can call him to God, but when a man is walking with God the Word can send him to do something for God.

When Ezekiel was concerned to know what God would have him say in prophesying to Israel, God in a vision used the figure of having Ezekiel eat the roll of a book. Ezekiel saw himself eat the roll which was filled with lamentations, and mourning and woe. When he digested what he had thus eaten he found it was in the mouth as honey for sweetness. In this way Ezekiel was being shown that while the truth was that Israel would have distress, yet knowing the truth would be a precious delight to Ezekiel.

In thus eating the Word of God there is pictured the personal nature of understanding the will of God. One aspect of eating is very obvious—each individual eats for himself! It is much like the Lord's Supper. Even though its observance may be a corporate action on the part of many, participation in it is single. The group never eats the bread! Each individual eats and swallows it for himself.

This has profound significance for the understanding of spiritual life and growth.

Another important truth is that the individual who eats and swallows the bread is actually committing himself and only himself to the consequences.

How is the Word of God like food to the soul (Matthew 4:4)? What aspect of Bible study is like a person eating a meal? If food gives strength, what is the kind of strength Bible study gives? How can erroneous teaching be compared with poisoned food? What might be the consequences? What changes could this lesson bring about in *your* personal life?

4. Sweeter Than Honey
Psalm 19:10

The Word of God is definitely a blessing to anyone who hears it in faith. When Ezekiel saw the roll of the book in his vision, the appearance was not reassuring (Ezekiel 2:10). But when he had eaten it he found it was "as honey for sweetness" (Ezekiel 3:3). The appearance was forbidding but getting to know what it meant was definitely desirable.

This is a truth which is experienced often in God's ways with men. It was a bitter experience for Joseph to be sold as a slave but it led to many lives being spared. The cross of Calvary was a shameful prospect but through it the Lord had the joy of obedience and of bringing many sons to glory.

The taste will remain unknown to all who do not partake. It is only those who eat the Word, who actually receive it into the heart to obey it, who can ever know that it is "sweeter than honey."

This is a profound insight into the nature of spiritual experience. Many aspects of the world are to be noted for what they are by outward observation. But it is quite different with the things of the Spirit and of the heart. These are inward and invisible.

The sweetness of the will of God is supplied by his mercy and grace. If the Word revealed concerns guidance or direction the believer should follow; it is sweet because the will of God is good and kind. Things will work out well and the believer can be assured of blessing. If the Word revealed concerns circumstances or what may happen to the believer he can rest assured. God doeth all things well.

When is any message welcome? Name the five persons whose fortunes and welfare mean the most to you. What do you fear most of all? What troubles you most about your family? What news could give you the greatest joy? What is the most precious promise in the Bible to you? What has this lesson meant to you?

5. Bought Without Money
Isaiah 55:2

Salvation is a blessing worth more than all the

money in the world. Money is useful only here and now. Yet there is so much even in this present life that money cannot buy. Some people have much joy who have no money to spend. On the other hand, some people have so much money they cannot find time or occasion to spend it all, but they have no joy. It is obvious that money is not the final answer to living.

Yet money can be very useful. Many material necessities and luxuries can be purchased with money. It is actually a handy condensation of human labor. It represents time and energy.

To say that money cannot buy everything is to say that man by his own efforts cannot secure everything. There are things that matter very much which a man cannot get by his own efforts. A man cannot make the sun shine, as important as this is in the natural world. A man cannot prolong life even one heartbeat when death has come. A man cannot force loyalty or friendship from people. And these are only some of the things money cannot buy.

Just so is the grace of God—this comes from Him. It is free from the heart of God. It is bestowed upon those who trust in Him and who receive Jesus Christ as Saviour.

The bridegroom does not buy the love of the bride. The child does not buy the love of his father. The country need not pay for the loyalty of its patriots.

The best things of life are free. The grace of God is to be had without money and without price.

What is the most important thing in your life? How much money are you spending on it? What would help our nation more than anything else? What is most important for a home? What bothers you today more than anything else? Name the four most important things money *can* buy. Name the four most important things money *cannot* buy. What difference does money make in your personal relationship with God?

6. The Bread of Life
   John 6:48

In a very real sense you are what you eat. Jesus of Nazareth told his disciples they would need to eat him that they might have eternal life. Certainly he was not referring to anything like cannibalism. But he was nonetheless referring to a very real sense in which the disciples would appropriate the things of Christ as their own. It would be a case of taking the person of Christ to be their own person.

Many of his disciples did not understand, or so far as they understood did not want, that pattern of living for themselves. They called his teaching "a hard saying" and began to turn away to seek their own.

His own disciples, however, were led by Peter to remain committed to him. They believed he was that Christ, the Son of the living God, and that he had the words of eternal life. In so doing they began to take to themselves, for themselves, what Christ Jesus was in himself.

As He was the Son of the living God, they

received "power to become the sons of God." As the words He spoke were Spirit and life (John 6:63), receiving what He said resulted in newness of life (John 5:24). Because God was His Father, they became the children of God. Because God has put all things in His hands, they became the heirs of God, joint heirs with Jesus Christ (Galatians 3:29; Romans 8:17). Because he would be raised from the dead, he would raise them from the dead (John 6:21-29).

Why is food so necessary for living? Where is food to be found? Do you have any responsibility for finding food? How important is supervision of food? Do you think pure food laws are an undesirable exercise of control? How does a child get its food? From the feeding of babies, what can we learn about teaching the Bible to children? What can we learn about the importance of Bible study by looking at the production and preparation of food?

7. Not by Bread Alone
Matthew 4:4

Man has both soul and body in which he lives and can be affected. The body is related to this world of nature. The soul is related to the other world of the Spirit. The interests of the body and the soul are not always identical, neither do they cover the same areas. Sometimes body and soul can actually be contrary to each other. Because the body belongs to the earth in a temporal way, and the soul belongs to heaven in an eternal way, the soul is much more important.

The Word of God deals directly with the soul. For this reason Jesus of Nazareth put obedience to the Word of God before the natural interest that his body had in food (Matthew 4:4). Paul in a similar way put his fleshly interests under restraint to have complete freedom for the interests of the soul (I Corinthians 8:13; 9:27). He believed this to be the standard procedure of all real believers (Galatians 5:24).

Jesus of Nazareth lived in total obedience to his Father, never allowing his flesh to take the initiative in anything. He set this pattern during the temptation in the wilderness, but he manifested it in a classic way in Gethsemane. Paul entered into this fellowship with Christ by denying himself (Galatians 2:20).

It is important for the believer to remember that he cannot follow Christ in his own strength. Any attempt to do this will result in failure and in deception. The believer will be defeated to the hurt of those about him unless he feeds on the Word of God and denies himself in spiritual service.

Is anything more important than food? What evidence can you call to mind that would show that food is not always the most important thing in a home? Can money alone guarantee rest and peace? How can you see that money is not essential to blessing? How can money bring blessing? Leaving out money, what is the most important thing you would want your child to have in life?

Make a Decision

"Taste and see that the Lord is good," says the psalmist. We taste the Lord by claiming what he has promised in his Word. All that man needs to save his soul and to build him up in the faith is to be found in God's Word, the Bible.

It has been said, and rightly so, that sin will keep you from the Bible and the Bible will keep you from sin.

Are you living a victorious Christian life? If not, could it be that you have not been feeding on the Word so that you will have the strength you need for the trials of the day?

CHAPTER 11

For You and Me

Bible reading for this week: Acts 2:38-40

The gospel of Jesus Christ has come into the world for all men. God is no respecter of persons. Whosoever will may come. The same message goes to all—whosoever believeth in Him hath everlasting life.

Yet men are saved one by one. In the Lord's Supper instruction is given to the worshipers that each one is to eat the bread and to drink the cup.

The Scriptures are given to all men, but they must be received by each one, and be believed in by the individual soul.

1. Abraham: "I will Bless Thee"
Genesis 12:2

The call of Abraham is recorded in the Bible in the very next chapter after the story of the Tower of Babel, and can best be understood when comparison is made between these two events. The Tower of Babel was a community project undertaken by the people as a group. The language is clear —Let us make brick, let us build us a city, let us make us a name, lest we be scattered. (See Genesis 11:3-9.) The call of Abraham was an individual matter—Get thee out of thy country, I will make of thee . . . , I will bless thee and make thy name great, and thou shall be a blessing (Genesis 12:1-3). The procedures were entirely different. The men of Babel planned to do the work as a community project; Abraham looked for a city whose builder and maker is God (Hebrews 11:10). The results were also exactly opposite. At Babel men began as a group and were scattered abroad; Abraham was called out from his people to a life of separation and through him all families of the earth are to be blessed.

The call to separation was the principle that marked the life of Abraham. His personal career began when he was called to come out from his kindred, his father's house, his native land into a land that God would show to him. Soon he was called to separate from his nephew Lot, which he arranged by giving Lot his choice of grazing lands. Some time later he faced the very painful separation from his own flesh when he sent away Ishmael with his mother Hagar. The climactic stage of his spiritual experience occurred when he offered up his son Isaac, in whom the promise was involved. In each of these experiences Abraham was personally being brought nearer to God.

What was the blessing of Abraham in New Testament language (Galatians 3:14)? List the benefits outlined to Abraham in the covenant (Genesis 12:1-3). Did Abraham need to do anything to receive this covenant (Hebrews 11:8-19)? Why? List what Abraham had to give up to obey the call of God. Why was the offering up of Isaac such a test of Abraham's faith? How do you think you would react to a similar test? How would you account for Abraham deceiving Abimelech about Sarah (Genesis 20:1-18)?

2. Jacob: "I will Keep Thee"
Genesis 28:15

Jacob is an outstanding illustration of the truth that a man does not need to scheme to receive the blessing of God. His natural disposition seemed to have been one of grasping to secure the benefits of God's favor. He drove a sharp bargain with Esau to secure the birthright. He collaborated with his mother Rebekah to deceive his aged father in order to gain the blessing which Isaac thought he was giving to Esau. But all this shady procedure was quite unnecessary. God had it in mind to bless him before he was born (Genesis 25:23).

Yet it does not seem necessary to hold that God's choice of Jacob was arbitrary. Paul discusses this to point out that God knew he would bless Jacob before the twins were born, having revealed his will when he gave the word, "Jacob have I loved, but Esau have I hated." But here Peter helps the understanding when he writes, "Elect according to the foreknowledge of God . . ." (I Peter 1:2).

In any case it seems that Jacob in himself had no assurance he would be blessed, even though such was the will of God. Here is an instance where God is able to do exceeding abundantly above all that we ask or think. (See Ephesians 3:20.)

At Bethel God distinctly promised Jacob that He would watch over him, would bring him back to the land through which he was going, and would give this land to him as an inheritance. This promise was for him and for him alone. God will bless all who trust in him, but each one in his own special way.

At Peniel Jacob was left alone and there he was lifted to the highest blessing of his life when God dealt with him, humbling him and blessing him in mercy and grace.

The reader of the Bible can look at Jacob as an example of what God will do for anyone who turns to him in Christ.

Contrast Jacob and Esau in the incident of the birthright (Genesis 25:29-34). How is the grace of God to be seen at Bethel (Genesis 26:10-22)? What steps did Jacob take to seek to escape the wrath of Esau (Genesis 32:3-8)? What was Jacob's argument in prayer to God for help (Genesis 32:9-12)? Recall an experience which involved you in personal danger. Did it drive you to "wrestle with God" in prayer? How did it affect your life?

3. Moses: "I Will Be With Thee"
Exodus 4:12

The gospel of Jesus Christ is offered to all men with a very simple formula—"Believe on the Lord Jesus Christ, and thou shalt be saved, and thy house" (Acts 16:31). This is valid for anybody anywhere at anytime. But the actual experience of being saved will vary in each case.

The gospel not only promises deliverance from this present evil world, but it calls people into communion with the Lord, and it commissions them into service for the Lord. It is here that variations occur, and differences begin to appear. The career of Moses for which he was prepared by providence and into which he was called by God would be unique. No one else would ever be the leader of Israel coming out of Egypt, marching across the desert and entering into the land of Canaan. Though most believers will live simple and obscure lives by comparison, the same principle of guidance will be involved.

The circumstances of Moses' call were unique in the burning bush that was not consumed, the rod that became a serpent, and the hand that became leprous. The incidents in his service were also unique in the series of plagues brought upon Egypt. The aspects of the proposal to compromise offered by Pharaoh arose out of the specific circumstances in which Moses and the Hebrews were involved, but the truth of such challenges and the significance of his faithfulness in rejecting the proposal are applicable to all believers everywhere.

How was faith implied in Miriam's standing nearby when Pharaoh's daughter found Moses? What seems to be the nature of the decision Moses had to make when he was "come to years" (Hebrews 11:24-26)? How did Moses have the wisdom or the courage to deny Pharaoh's attempts to make him compromise? In what various ways was Moses prepared for his service? Trace so far as you can God's providence in preparing you for your present work.

4. Joshua: "I Will Magnify Thee"
Joshua 1:5

The call of God brings men into situations which may be much more important than they ever knew or expected. The actual service a believer may give to the Lord may owe much of its significance to circumstances about which the servant had little or perhaps nothing to do. Joshua had been Moses' servant, and a military commander to whom Moses gave specific tasks. Upon the death of Moses, Joshua was suddenly put in the place of Moses to be the leader of all the people in the great movement of the Exodus.

For the new responsibilities God gave Joshua new power. This was done by giving him specific promises so that he could meet the new and greater demands he must face. Also he was given specific commandment and exhortation as to how he must take up his task. And he was assured that God would magnify him in the eyes of all the people who were to accept him as leader and follow his guidance.

In this a profound truth is revealed. The prestige any man may have at any time is not so much the result of what he has done, is doing or will do, as much as it is the result of a willingness on the part of the public to esteem this man as being great. But then he must live up to the esteem—he must be able to meet the needs of the hour.

Any leader needs to have the inclination of the people to follow him. They must accept him as worthy and able and have confidence in his judgment to commit themselves to follow him. It was not so much what Joshua actually was in himself, though that would be very important to him, but it was what they thought of him that measured the service he could render.

How would it help us to understand that Joshua was a man of faith before he was called to take Moses' place? How was his faith challenged when God called him to lead Israel? What aspect of the charge he was given called for faith in Joshua before any results were to be seen? When the army was defeated at Ai why did Joshua not rebuke the commanders (Joshua 7:6-9)? What is implied in

Joshua 7:10-15 about the proper procedure in dealing with sin? Why did Joshua make the unfortunate alliance with Gibeon (Joshua 9:3-15)?

5. David: "I Will Build Thy House"
II Samuel 7:16

The gospel of Jesus Christ brings the promise of blessing by the grace of God. It belongs to the glory of God that he will choose "the weak things of the world to confound the things which are mighty" (I Corinthians 1:27). Jesus of Nazareth in public prayer gave thanks to his Father "because thou hast hid these things from the wise and prudent, and hast revealed them unto babes" (Matthew 11:25). Gideon found it hard to believe that God would use him to save Israel since "my family is poor in Manasseh, and I am the least in my father's house" (Judges 6:15). Nathan reminded David how the Lord took him from the sheepcote, from following the sheep, to be ruler over His people, over Israel (II Samuel 7:8). David himself was very conscious of this amazing display of grace: "Who am I, O Lord God? and what is my house, that thou hast brought me hitherto" (II Samuel 7:18)? Throughout the Bible this principle is illustrated over and over that all praise and honor should belong to God, and "no flesh should glory in his presence" (I Corinthians 1:29).

The grace of God is seen not only in the choice of the servant He will use, but also in the blessing with which He helps the servant in his service. In providence David had the opportunity to face Goliath. By the grace of God he had the courage to use his skill to kill the enemy.

When he was in Saul's house he was given a wonderful friend in Jonathan. In his conflict with Saul, David was helped in providence to avoid Saul. Also he was given wonderful help in the mighty men who came to serve under his leadership.

How is the grace of God to be seen in His choice of David? Do you think God knew that David would sin in the matter of Uriah the Hittite before he made his covenant with him? Name five of David's friends and account for the friendship of each. Name three of David's enemies and account for the hostility of each. List the troubles David had in his family.

6. Peter: "I Will Make You Fishers of Men"
Matthew 4:19

The blessing of God comes to believers in various ways. To be able to believe is a gift from God. To be called to serve Him is by the grace of God. To have His help in providence that the service be effectual is by the goodness of God. Now we are to see that the inner changes of character are also by the grace of God.

Peter, James and John were fishermen and as such would never have been thought of as teachers or preachers. Jesus of Nazareth called them to serve Him. Later when Peter and John were brought into court because of their activity as witnesses for their resurrected Lord, people marveled when they saw their boldness even though they "perceived that they were unlearned and ignorant men" (Acts 4:13).

When Jesus of Nazareth chose His twelve disciples He had in mind that they would be prepared for their ministry (Matthew 10:1). When He taught the multitude using parables, He explained to His disciples more fully the truth He had been illustrating. When He performed His great miracles He took Peter, James and John with Him that they might see His power and the truth.

Before He left this world He taught His disciples many things. Thus He demonstrated the humility they should exercise when He washed the disciples feet. He refused to shrink from the cross and taught them to expect suffering.

What evidence is there that Peter was impulsive? What evidence is there that Peter was unstable? What evidence is there that Peter loved Jesus of Nazareth? What evidence is there that Peter was one of those closest to Jesus personally? Why did Peter object to Jesus' washing his feet? Did Peter suspect that Judas Iscariot was dishonest? Comment. What does it mean to you personally that God does deal with each person individually? List some personal dealings you have had with God.

7. Paul: "I Will Send Thee"
Acts 9:4

The apostle Paul always felt that he had personally received the grace of God in a special way that he should be an example to others who would come to faith (I Timothy 1:16). Certainly the truth of the gospel was brought into Paul's soul in dramatic fashion on the Damascus road. Such an unusual experience might not be repeated, but the truth that the Lord calls the sinner to Himself is for everyone in the gospel.

Paul's personal experience of the grace of God was the source of his clear understanding of the spiritual life that was possible in Christ Jesus. This he felt was given to him as a trust that he must share with all men everywhere in any way he could (Romans 1:14,15). His record of service and the testimony even of his enemies that he had turned the world upside down (Acts 17:6) will always be a monument to the zeal and the wisdom with which he preached the gospel.

Part of his power and dedication was due to the fact that Paul knew so well that the gospel he presented was not his own, nor was it of any human origin (Galatians 1:11,12). Also he knew in his own heart that his going from place to place preaching was not his own idea (II Corinthians 1:12). He was obedient to the guidance of the Lord in that which he did (II Corinthians 1:17 and note also Acts 16:6-10).

What evidence is there that Paul was a respected

man among the Jews before he accepted Christ Jesus? What evidence is there that the Jews turned against Paul when he became a Christian? Why did Paul quote a Greek poet when he spoke to the Athenians on Mars Hill (Acts 17:22-31)? Give your views on the wisdom of this approach. Since Paul knew that circumcision was not necessary, why did he have Timothy circumcised (Acts 16:1-5)? Why did Paul agree to share in a Jewish vow (Acts 21:20-26)? Why did Paul return thanks to God for food in the presence of pagans (Acts 27:35)?

Make a Decision

"Behold, I stand at the door, and knock: if any man hear my voice, and open the door, I will come in to him, and will sup with him, and he with me" (Revelation 3:20).

In this study we have seen what God will do for and with the one who opens his heart's door and lets Him have full control of his life.

Abraham was blessed mightily and through him others too were blessed. This will always be true for those who commit their lives to him. Do you know the joy and fellowship of the Lord in your daily life? Name the ways.

CHAPTER 12

To Tell the World

Bible reading for this week: Luke 24:44-53

The gospel of Jesus Christ is for the whole world. In recent years the public has begun to refer to "one world," but this is not new to the thinking of the Christian. More recently public reference is frequently made to the truth of social interrelations among all men. This is not anything new to the Scriptures. Nearly two thousand years ago Paul affirmed on Mars Hill: "God that made the world and all things therein . . . hath made of one blood all nations of men for to dwell on all the face of the earth" (Acts 17:24-26).

When the Lord Jesus instructed his disciples with the great commission He put the whole world within the focus of Christian responsibility.

1. All Things Are of God
Genesis 2:1,2

"I believe in God the Father Almighty, Maker of heaven and earth." This is a time-honored affirmation of Christians. "No man hath seen God at any time." Who then is God? What is He like? First of all, he is the Creator. It is He who brought all things into being. He is the Maker. He is the Designer. It is His wisdom, His strength, His power that make and that keep all things as they are.

All power belongs to God. Everything that moves, that lives, does so because God makes it possible. He not only empowers all that happens but He guides the course of events.

All things are known to God. He knows the end from the beginning. He not only knows everything that has happened, but He knows all the infinite variety of things that could have happened. In that sense He is in on everything that happens. This is not to say that what happened is what He wanted, but it is to say that nothing could happen without His permission.

In providence God sets up things in such a way that certain things may just naturally happen, and certain other things just cannot happen. For example, if there is no lake or river anywhere around children will not go swimming and will not drown. There is a sense in which through providence God channels the flow of possible events. Even when things that are possible are happening, God in providence can overrule by introducing some other factor.

Any person is really blessed who can believe that "God doeth all things well."

What are some of the natural problems arising out of the fact that God overrules everything that happens? What are some of the assurances grounded in the fact that God controls all that happens? How will such a view affect the outlook in praying? How will such a view affect the significance of this world? How does this view support the idea of predictive prophecy? Give one experience in your own life when you were guided in providence to make the right decision.

2. Judgments of God
II Peter 3:7

Because God is a living God, and because He knows all things, he is the Judge of all the earth. Because He is holy, and of purer eyes than to behold evil, His judgment is just. It is His purpose to destroy evil. He warned Adam from the very first that the soul that sins shall die.

Again and again things happen that are not in accord with God's precepts. In the plant world the organisms which do contrary to the implicit design wither and die. When this occurs in the animal world there may be conflict as well as sickness and death.

Because God is a God of grace He warns man of the peril in disobeying His will. Then He also provides a way of escape. In judgment God remembers mercy and arranges that sinning man can be forgiven and reinstated in His good will.

Because God knew that man would sin and thus be doomed to die, God in mercy provided a Saviour who could and would at the cost of His own life save all who would receive him as Saviour and Lord.

In the saving work of the Messiah the Law of God is fully honored. If I commit a traffic violation that brings a fine of forty dollars, the only way to honor the law is for me to be assessed a fine for forty dollars. If some friend of mine steps forward and pays the forty dollars, the law is fully honored though I now go free. I am as free as if I had never broken that law.

What affect will it have on the mind of a man if he believes God is his judge? Why would the judgment of God necessarily be true? Why does this doctrine not keep men from doing evil? How would the upbringing of children affect their later acceptance of this doctrine? How does it affect your personal life that God is the Judge of all the earth?

3. All Nations Will Be Blessed in the Seed of Abraham
Genesis 12:3

"All have sinned, and come short of the glory of God" (Romans 3:23). ". . . and so death passed upon all men, for that all have sinned" (Romans 5:12).

The world is in trouble. Not only because men are weak and ignorant and unfortunate, but because they are sinful and do wrong. Men are hurting men all over the world. No one knows what to do and things are getting worse.

The Bible offers a solution to the problem of living in this world. Abraham was the pioneer of living by faith. When all other men were scheming to meet the problem by getting together in community action apart from God, Abraham looked to the Lord for help. While the men of Babel planned to build a city by their own efforts, Abraham "looked for a city which hath foundations, whose builder and maker is God" (Hebrews 11:10).

Through the Scriptures this procedure is shown again and again. When confronted by an impossible situation believing men have turned to God and have been helped through to victory because they trusted in Him.

This is the way of the gospel of Jesus Christ and it is always the way to blessing. Jesus of Nazareth told his hearers that He personally did nothing on His own. He always obeyed His Father and since God held all things in His hands, Jesus in obeying His Father was actually attending to every need in any situation.

The prophets foretold of the future day when all the kingdoms of the world would become the kingdoms of the Messiah. In that day this blessed procedure would prevail in every way.

What does this prophecy show about how God looks at different people, races, and the like? Does this mean that all men will have the same experience? Does this mean that God looks at all men in the same way? Explain: "God is not willing that any should perish." Explain: "Many are called but few are chosen." What new truth have you learned from this study?

4. The Throne of David Shall Be Established Forever
II Samuel 7:13

The covenant with Abraham promised that in his seed all nations would be blessed. The covenant with David repeated that promise with something specific added. The blessing of Abraham will take the form of the kingdom of the Son of David.

Paul implied that the blessing of Abraham would mean receiving "the promise of the Spirit through faith" (Galatians 3:14). The implication seems to be that the Holy Spirit will establish the Kingdom of God in the soul of the believer. This seems to be what is meant when it is written "He shall take of mine, and shall show it unto you" (John 16:15).

The very meaning of the title "Christ" points to the Lord being "King." Since God has given Him a name which is above every name (Philippians 2:9), being King He must be King of kings, and His throne must be over all other thrones. This is exactly what the covenant with David promised to the seed of David.

When the believer receives Christ Jesus as Saviour and Lord, God sends the Holy Spirit into his heart (Galatians 4:6). The Holy Spirit writes the law of God upon the heart so that the believer will inwardly want to do the will of God (Hebrews 8:10). In this way the Holy Spirit activates the will of Jesus Christ in the believer (Philippians 2:13). So even in this sense the throne of David is actually being established for eternity.

Does this mean there will be no disobedient or rebelling elements in the whole of creation? How will Christ establish his control over Satan? What does this imply about living, dynamic elements in creation? Do you think the throne of David and the great white throne are identical? (See Revelation 20.) How far will the authority of the throne of David extend? (See II Samuel 7.) How long will the throne of David continue its reign? (Hebrews 1:8.) What has this lesson meant to you?

5. All Nations Shall Yield to Messiah's Rule
Isaiah 2:2

The gospel of Jesus Christ deals first with the individual. Men are called to believe in Christ one by one and are transformed by the grace of God as the Holy Spirit activates the will of Christ, the living Word of God in their hearts according to the new covenant.

But these regenerated persons live for the most part in nations. The prophets looked to a day when the Kingdom of God would finally overcome all the kingdoms of this world. And people of all nations

141

would flow into God's Kingdom. Gone would be the times when the Gentiles were forbidden to enter the courts of the temple of Jerusalem.

When prophets like Isaiah looked into the future they saw the establishing of the Kingdom of God as one great, inclusive social structure in which peace would prevail. Such peace would not be imposed by arbitrary coercion but would be the result of the wise rule of Messiah over subjects who would voluntarily come to him to yield to his control (Isaiah 2:2-4).

When sin entered the human race through Adam's fall, man became conscious of self and was filled with a disposition to act independently as he pleased. This led to conflict among men, even as with Cain's killing of Abel because he hated him for being preferred before him. The grace of God in Christ Jesus leads to self-denial and fills the heart with love toward others.

Who do you think are "all nations" (Isaiah 2:2)? Did Jesus of Nazareth ever address the Roman Nation? Did any of the apostles ever preach to any nation or city as such? How shall we understand Old Testament messages being sent to nations whereas the New Testament does not do this? Explain Philippians 2:9-11.

6. All Men Should Repent
Acts 17:30

The Bible says simply, "... all have sinned, and

come short of the glory of God" (Romans 3:23). This means not only that they have done wrong, but it means also that they have become wrong. Now they are sinful. There is no man that does not sin. (See Ecclesiastes 7:20.)

Salvation must not only take away the sins which men commit, but must also deliver man from the sinfulness that is now in him.

When Jesus Christ came to save He came not only to bear away the sins of men in His own body, but He came to redeem man from the bondage into which He was born as a human being. It was by His personal dying in the flesh, being buried and being raised in newness of life that this could be done and was done. Now the sinner can be saved—spirit, soul and body—through Christ Jesus.

But such salvation is possible only in and through and by Jesus Christ. The sinner must come to Christ and receive him as Saviour and Lord. This involves a personal yielding to Christ following genuine repentance. Repentance involves judgment upon self.

Repentance is not only being sorry for sins. Sins are no doubt awful and being sorry is quite appropriate, but this alone is not repentance. Nor is repentance a matter of promising to do better. It is actually a matter of self appraisal in which a sinner sees himself as being truly a sinner who is worthy of being condemned. He knows he needs to be changed. He turns from sin and turns toward God.

When the Bible is taken as a mirror and the sinner sees himself as he is, such a soul can turn to Christ in surrender to accept salvation in Him.

Why is simply being sorry for wrongdoing not an adequate procedure? Why is promising to do better not really adequate for dealing with wrongdoing? What promise in the Gospel holds out hope for an adequate treatment of my disposition to do wrong? What is the basic reason why anybody would turn away from Christ and his offer to save? What is the weakness in preaching which dwells upon the rewards of virtue? What is the weakness in preaching which dwells upon the punishment of vice? What should preaching dwell upon?

7. All Men Should Receive Jesus Christ
John 6:29; Acts 4:12

Every man is responsible to God who is His Creator, Keeper and Judge. This is the only world a man can live in and die in. No man has any other alternative. And this world was made by God, is kept by God, and will be judged by God. Man must face God to give an account of the deeds of the body. Every man must give account to God for every idle word he has spoken.

God knows that all the world is guilty before Him, and in His compassion He has arranged a way of escape. "God so loved the world, that he gave his only begotten Son, that whosoever believeth in him should not perish, but have everlasting life" (John 3:16). This presents man with a very simple issue. There really is just one thing for him to do.

When Jesus of Nazareth went about teaching and

preaching the Kingdom of God, men knew He came from God to tell them the truth. On one occasion they asked him, "What shall we do, that we might work the works of God" (John 6:28)? His answer was plain and direct: "This is the work of God, that ye believe on him whom he hath sent" (John 6:29). By believing on Christ Jesus the soul is committed to God, thus to receive from Him the grace that will save.

"Seek ye first the Kingdom of God, and his righteousness; and all these things shall be added unto you" (Matthew 6:33).

Why is the message about Jesus Christ called the gospel? What is implied in the fact there is but one gospel to be preached to all men everywhere? How is it possible that the message is still valid even though things in the world have changed so much? Give four illustrations of basic relationships that have not changed since Bible times. Give four illustrations of radical changes that have occurred in human experience. Do these affect the basic relationship between God and man? Why? What effect does it have upon the mind of man that there is one gospel for all men?

Make a Decision

The gospel of Jesus Christ is for you. Once you have received Christ Jesus into your heart as your Saviour and Lord He will call you to be His witness. He will guide you and give you power to be an effective witness as you yield your life completely into His keeping. Jesus Christ said, "Ye shall receive power, after that the Holy Ghost is come upon you: and ye shall be witnesses unto me . . . unto the uttermost part of the earth."

Do you know Jesus Christ? If so are you telling others what great things the Lord hath done for you?

Books for Further Study

BRUCE, F. F. *The Books and the Parchments: Some Chapters on the Transmission of the Bible.* Westwood, N. J.: Revell, 1963.

BRUCE, F. F. *The English Bible: A History of Translations.* New York: Oxford, 1961.

BRUCE, F. F. *The New Testament Documents: Are They Reliable?* Grand Rapids: Eerdmans, 1960. Paperback.

CRUDEN, ALEXANDER. *Cruden's Concordance.* This Bible concordance is available from several publishers in abridged and unabridged editions.

DAVIDSON, FRANCIS, editor. *The New Bible Commentary.* Grand Rapids: Eerdmans, 1953.

DOUGLAS, J. D., organizing editor. *The New Bible Dictionary.* Grand Rapids: Eerdmans, 1962.

GROLLENBERG, LUCAS H. *Atlas of the Bible.* New York: Nelson, 1956.

HALLEY, HENRY H. *Halley's Bible Handbook.* Grand Rapids: Zondervan, 1966.

HARRISON, EVERETT F. and PFEIFFER, CHARLES F., editors. *The Wycliffe Bible Commentary.* Chicago: Moody, 1962.

HENRY, CARL F. H., consulting editor. *The Biblical Expositor.* Philadelphia: Lippincott, 1960.

HENRY, CARL F. H. *Christian Personal Ethics.* Grand Rapids: Eerdmans, 1957.

HENRY, CARL F. H., editor. *Revelation and the Bible.* Grand Rapids: Baker, 1958.

LA SOR, WILLIAM S. *Amazing Dead Sea Scrolls and the Christian Faith.* Chicago: Moody, 1956.

MEARS, HENRIETTA C. *What the Bible Is All About*. Glendale, Calif.: G/L Regal, 1966.

MICKELSEN, A. BERKELEY. *Interpreting the Bible*. Grand Rapids: Eerdmans, 1963.

PFEIFFER, CHARLES F., editor. *The Biblical World: A Dictionary of Biblical Archaeology*. Grand Rapids: Baker, 1966.

PFEIFFER, CHARLES F. and VOS, HOWARD F. *The Wycliffe Historical Geography of Bible Lands*. Chicago: Moody, 1967.

RAMM, BERNARD. *Special Revelation and the Word of God*. Grand Rapids: Eerdmans, 1961.

The Sacred Land. Chicago: FIELD ENTERPRISES EDUCATIONAL CORP., 1966. (Historical maps from before 1500 B. C. to present day.)

SMITH, WILBUR. *Profitable Bible Study*. Natick, Mass.: Wilde, 1963.

THOMPSON, J. A. *The Bible and Archaeology*. Grand Rapids: Eerdmans, 1962.

TENNEY, MERRILL C. *New Testament Survey*. Grand Rapids: Eerdmans, 1961.

TENNEY, MERRILL C. *The Zondervan Pictorial Bible Dictionary*. Grand Rapids: Zondervan, 1963.

WALVOORD, JOHN F., editor. *Inspiration and Interpretation*. Grand Rapids: Eerdmans, 1957.

YOUNG, EDWARD J. *Thy Word Is Truth*. Grand Rapids: Eerdmans, 1957. Paperback.

YOUNG, EDWARD J. *An Introduction to the Old Testament*. Grand Rapids: Eerdmans, 1958.